EIGHT BELLS
YARNS OF THE WATCH

EIGHT BELLS
YARNS OF THE WATCH

and some
STORIES OF MY LIFE

CHARLES TRELEAVEN

Copyright © Charles Treleaven 2021
Cover design, Typesetting: Working Type Studio
(www.workingtype.com.au)

The right of Charles Treleaven to be identified as the Author of the Work has been asserted in accordance with the Copyright, Designs and Patents Act 1988.

All rights reserved. No part of this publication may be reproduced, stored in a retrieval system, or transmitted in any form or by any means without the prior written permission of the publisher, nor be otherwise circulated in any form of binding or cover other than that in which it is published and without a similar condition being imposed on the subsequent purchaser.

Charles Treleaven
Eight Bells: Yarns of the Watch
ISBN: 978-0-6452041-5-5

Contents

Foreword to Memoirs	1
PART ONE: PRE AND POST WORLD WAR II	**5**
1. Early Memories of the World in the 1930's	7
2. My Wartime Boyhood and the Blitz on London	17
3. The Post World War Two Period.	29
PART TWO: MY YEARS AT SEA	**41**
4. Why I Chose the Merchant Navy	43
5. Tramping the World	47
6. The Leaving of Liverpool	49
7. My first foreign seaport — Alexandria in Egypt.	59
8. Alexandria to Marseilles (Christmas — 1948)	67
9. The Christmas Storm	71
10. Marseilles to Saigon	77
11. Loading rice in Bangkok	89
12. Ceylon (Sri Lanka) 1950	91
13. My return to England.	97
14. Durban — South Africa	103
15. Durban to Hong Kong	107
16. Nauru. (Gilbert & Ellice Islands)	109
17. Nauru to Australian Ports	113
18. The Maritime Menagerie.	117
19. The Crickets at Portarlington	131
20. Port Lincoln. (And the ship " Mill Hill ")	137
21. Calcutta — Refit and Coal for Melbourne	141

22. Melbourne in the Early Fifties	145
23. Loading Grain in Willlamstown	151
24. Loading copra in the Philippine Islands for USA	157
25. Loading for Korean War	165
26. Auckland to Liverpool	169
27. The Loss Of HMS Affray	173
28. Ghent — What is in a Name.	177
29. Ghent to Newport News, & Puerto Rico.	179
30. Loading sugar in The Dominican Republic	183
31. At Portuguese Marmagoa.	187
32. Morma Goa to Rotterdam	195
33. The Unexpected trip to Matardi, Belgian Congo.	201
34. Ashore for my 2nd Mates Certificate	205
35. The King Edward Seventh Navigation School	207
36. Leadenhall Street in the Fifties.	221
37. New Zealand Shipping Company	227
38. Union Shipping Co. of New Zealand	241
39. Oceanographic Ship "Taranui"	249
40. With a Song in my Heart	261
41. The Magic Letter	269
42. The British Phosphate Commission	275
PART THREE: MY LIFE ASHORE	281
43. Lumacell Plastics Pty. Ltd.	283
44. The Citizens' Action Group	289
45. Inaugral Melbourne to Hobart Yacht Race — 1972.	293
46. In Jordan for the United Nations	297
47. My trip as a Tourist to South America.	307
48. My time at the Polly Woodside	315
The View from 2020	335
49. The Replica of Schooner 'Enterprize'.	337
50. The Maritime Heritage Association of Victoria, (MHAV)	343
51. Starlab & Teaching Astronomy.	351

Foreword to Memoirs

Why does a person write notes, even pages, about themselves? Probably it is some form of egotism, or a feeling that we need to make ourselves in some way special, even immortal. Is that the motivation?

However, one of the disappointments in my own life is that I know so little about my own father, and I hope that by these stories from my own life my children will at least have some record, and need not feel the same. They may not care, nor bother to read it, that's a risk, but at least it's available.

I naturally hope that they will all have some happy memories of times we have spent together. This will vary with the family groupings, because situations and opportunities change with age, occupation, and a slow maturing of the restless, unfulfilled spirit that lies within each person.

Some memories may be happy and some full of regrets and sadness, but perhaps my story may enable some understanding of events.

I went away to sea, not only to find adventure, but to escape the feeling of being a visitor in what was supposed to be my home. I really was only a boy at sixteen, but thrust into a man's world, with all its frailties, down to earth realities, and its generally critical attitude of society. I now blame these factors for the reason for my various marriage failures.

Now at the tail end of my brief stay on this planet, also I realise that this was the cause of my transience character, a need for reaching out for the permanence that I have never actually found — the grass is somewhere greener. By being a wanderer, I now pay the price by being lonely.

All of us have skeletons in the cupboard. These are to be regretted, and I certainly have more than perhaps my share, and while these may live in the memories of the less generous, I have not dwelt on them.

Our friend Shakespeare summed it up when he wrote — "The evil that men do lives after them. The good so often interred with their bones"

In general terms, I believe it comes back to being either an optimist or a pessimist, the 'old half full' or 'half empty story'. These basic traits influence every aspect of our lives and our reaction to the situations and challenges we face along life's way. We all have setbacks. It's how we handle them and then move on, that really matters.

I am not a trained philosopher nor even a particularly deep thinker — I wish I were — but in thinking of my own voyage down the years, I feel blessed that I am, more than anything, a 'half full' person. Once something that is unchangeable has happened, we should learn the lesson perhaps, but don't fret...you can't change yesterday.

I seem to remember something from Shakespeare about 'grasping the nettle'. Perhaps that's what I am doing in writing all this.

I hope you find it interesting.

Charles Treleaven.
February 2021.

HISTORICAL NOTE: The ringing of Eight Bells aboard a ship always signifies the end of a Watch. This goes back to a time before the invention of the chronometer, and the only visible time-keeper for a ship at sea was the Sun at its highest altitude when on the Meridian.

This occurs everywhere at Noon or 12 o'clock Apparent Time, and Eight Bells were made to announce the end of the old day and the start of a new.

PART ONE.

Events prior to Second World War

Memories of the World in the 30's.

Preparation for War.

Wartime boyhood memories and the Blitz on London.

Wartime Sequels.

Post-War Britain.

1. Early Memories of the World in the 1930's

It was a time of international economic difficulty, and unprecedented social confusion. The world was in the grips of the Great Depression. It was only fourteen years after the Great War concluded and those who fought for a better world were disillusioned that the promised prosperity was not at hand.

The year 1932 was infamous for important and troublesome events. Rutherford split the atom, Hitler came to power, and I was born. I am assured that my arrival was not the cause of my maternal Grandfather's premature demise, who died four months after I was born. When I was born my father was away on business and my mother was taken to hospital on the back of a stranger's motor bicycle.

European countries were close to following the example of Russia in 1919, with workers' revolution as a real possibility. In England workers were calling General Strikes and bringing the nation to a standstill. Troops had been called out to stop the workers rioting and marching on London. Bankruptcy was rife, including that of my maternal

Grandfather. A lifelong, celebrated Fleet Street journalist, a previous editor of the Daily Mail, and a Freeman of the City of London, William Monkton had financially guaranteed a friend's business that had failed. I am assured that it was this, and not my arrival, that caused his death soon after my birth, a broken man with a broken heart.

All over the world, idealists, the "Greenies" of the thirties, were leading the world to disarmament, while Hitler was laying his plans for opposing Communism with his National Socialism (Fascism) and preparing military revenge for the humiliation of the Treaty of Versailles, which had stripped Germany of both its pride, and its wealth by reparations.

That Treaty also lead to the formation of the League of Nations, a toothless tiger formed by the victorious Nations, but which proved useless in reining in the ambitions of the upcoming Military Dictatorships in Germany, Italy, and Japan. There was just not the will and courage to oppose the growing might of these emerging, re-arming Powers with their religion of Fascism. Fascist politicians started talking about war, imprisoning those that opposed them, and burning books that talked about democracy.

This period of appeasement led to World War Two which started in 1939. I do partially subscribe in retrospect that Prime Minister Chamberlin had actually bought us a year of peace in the preparation for war, by appeasing Hitler with his "Peace in our time" message. It was in this year that Britain developed its radar stations, equipped the public with gas masks and air-raid shelters, and armed the RAF with more fighter planes. Hitler had given advance notice of his intentions to expand the frontiers of Germany into Eastern Europe, and did not believe Britain and France would go to war. He had already taken over many countries, where he made claim that minority German populations were being persecuted. As far as the Allies were concerned, his invasion of Poland proved to be the last straw. (In 2019, Russia is claiming a similar situation, and now there's a rising China making similar statements)

(A pre-emptive strike, like that on Iraq in 2004, instead of the passive evacuation of the Rhineland by France and Britain in 1936, might have changed history and saved millions of lives)

Throughout the Thirties there was only a lone voice warning of the realism yet to come. That was the voice of Winston Churchill, and it was to him that the Commonwealth turned when they stood alone against the Nazi Axis in the Darkness of 1940.

Unemployment during the 1930's meant that one in three families in England and Australia had no income, and there was little financial help available. European countries were close to following the 1919 example of Russia, with workers' revolution as a real possibility. In England workers were calling General Strikes and bringing the nation to a standstill. Troops were called out to stop the workers rioting and marching on London. In Germany, National

Socialism stopped that happening and this was encouraged by a rebirth of National ambition and a sense of purpose.

This period of appeasement led to World War Two which started in 1939, even though the first German concentration camps for Jews were established as early as 1933. Jewish people were suffering terrible persecution throughout Germany and were leaving for England and USA if they could raise enough money.

This was the World into which I was nurtured.

Although of Cornish origins, I was brought up in Thornton Heath, Surrey, a dormitory suburb of London, and actually part of Croydon in Surrey. It lies about 33 miles South of London, sitting astride the old London to Brighton Highway. We later moved closer to London, to a suburb known as Streatham, in 1943.

I think my earliest memories go back to about 1934 when I was two years old. I remember that I was mad keen on Cowboys and Indians and would sit astride the arms of the living room couch riding my horse at breakneck speed, or riding an imaginary horse (a garden broom) and wearing Dad's pith helmet brought home as a relic of his cavalry time while in the Arabian Desert in 1917 fighting the Turks. Like Lawrence, he was posted there after being wounded at Gallipoli.

I also remember stopping at an uncle's home during a trip into the countryside in 1936 and viewing for the first time the early BBC television. Those early TV's had a screen about five inches in diameter, and the BBC ran just a couple of hours a day for experiments. These assisted the development of radar, and later the radar stations on the Coasts helped the RAF to defeat the Germans during the Battle of Britain. I have never understood why the Germans did not destroy those towers in the early stages of the war — I suppose they never understood their significance.

At the time we were living next to the Police Station, because the "plods" as we called them, would come in for a yarn and to share my father's whisky. They would keep me quiet by their heavy "Bobby" helmets pinning me to the carpet. My father was running his own business in textiles and theatre design during those terrible Depression years, and not doing too well. These were difficult times. It was either a feast or a famine, and occasionally we had no electricity or gas because bills had not been paid, so it was lucky we had both. When necessary, we passed our furniture over the back fence, to keep it from the hands of the bailiff.My earliest memories? Watching mother lighting the gas lights, when the electricity had been cut off — we thought it was great having both, but those fragile gas mantles had to be handled very carefully. Having my chest rubbed in front of the open fire by Grandma using warmed camphorated oil. Sitting on my father's shoulders in 1937 watching the sky lit up from the burning Crystal Palace. (A sight to be repeated when the Germans fire bombed the City of London during the Blitz in December 1941)

In 1938 when I started school — I can recall a bleak rainy day that matched my tears as I farewelled my mother at the school gate.

Preparations for War.

I was fitted with a gas mask. It was packed in a little cardboard box and made to be carried around at all times. This was about the time of the Munich crisis of 1938, and when we had the rising of international tensions during 1939.

Uncles turning up in uniform as Reservists were mobilised, and Father making our living room into a "citadel" with timber shores holding the ceiling, and blankets at the doors and windows, ready to be doused with water in the event of a gas attack. Detailed instructions for this engineering architectural masterpiece were found in the morning newspapers. Poison gas had been used during WW1, and it was thought to be a disastrous weapon to be used against civilian populations in the forth-coming conflict. (In actual fact it was never used by either side during WW2.)The citadel was actually made redundant by the delivery of an 'Anderson' air-raid shelter. It was made from a few curved pieces of heavy corrugated steel and required a hole dug in the back garden of about two metres square by one metre deep. The shelter was erected in the hole, with the dug-out soil covering the roof, and often

Anderson Shelter in back garden

making a modest rockery or flower bed, latterly used for growing vegetables when food became in short supply. We had the luxury of a rug over the concrete floor, and a kerosene heater. The shelter was furnished with twin bunks either side, and one across the back. We had a little hook-on table for our homework or for the countless hours of playing Monopoly by lantern light during the Blitz. During those months of bombing, life took on the routine of camping in the Anderson every night, and dashing for it during the daylight raids of the Battle of Britain when the schools were closed. We peered through the little door at the dog fights overhead, fought by those brave young men — "The Few" as they became known.

Those people without a garden, such as those living in flats, were issued with what became known as a 'Morrison Shelter'. This was in the form of a steel dining room table, that would protect those sheltering from the ruins of a collapsed building, and who could be afterwards rescued.

I remember a late breakfast on the September Sunday morning that war was declared — I was eating mashed bananas and cream. We listened to Chamberlain's bleak message on the family wireless, mother burst into tears, then the sudden warbling of air raid sirens sounding, replacing the noise of neighbours' lawn mowers. We kids were packed into the citadel with high emotion, but without the water being thrown on the curtains. The All Clear sounded very soon afterwards, and we have never known

Morrison Shelter

if there was a real threat of enemy bombers or just the Authorities making sure we knew hostilities had started.

I can remember the comments made by my parents. My father said "Bloody Germans — will they never learn." My mother, who had memories of being bombed by the German airships, the Zeppelins, in 1915, was really quite forthright. "The only good German is a dead German." I learnt how wrong this was many years later.

And so we went to war, and that was probably about the last banana eaten by me for many years.

<u>An Aside</u>: Many years later when I was running the Melbourne Maritime Museum, we commemorated the fiftieth anniversary of the war's outbreak with a special exhibition. Part of this was to gather ordinary people's memories of the day it all began. One lady rang me and asked "You want to know what I was doing at the moment war was declared?" Yes, I answered. "Well, mind your own bloody Business!" was all I was told.

Typical street scene after an air raid.

2. My Wartime Boyhood and the Blitz on London

I do have some other memories of those years of the war. It must have been terribly worrying for parents, but I frankly was too young to realise the seriousness of our situation, particularly after the evacuation at Dunkirk and during the Battle of Britain — when Britain and the Commonwealth stood alone against the power of Nazi Germany.

It was to be a Total War with the civilian community mobilised as well as the armed forces. Because of his rank and experience during WW1, Dad became Commander of the local LDV (Local Defence Volunteers) which in time became a true fighting force called the Home Guard (or Dad's Army), but in those early days, Dad would send men off to guard bridges armed only with broom sticks.

Mum was routinely on duty as a Fire Watcher, with her stirrup pump and bucket of sand, while my elder brother, with bicycle, was an Air Raid Messenger in case local communications broke down.

Mother was also working by day for the Red Cross who took over a magnificent house in Grosvenor Square, where I used to go to work during school holidays. London after Dunkirk was full of the strange uniforms of all the Free Forces of the nations invaded by the Nazis — Dutch, Belgians, French, Poles, Norwegians, Danes, etc, all of whom had exciting stories to tell of escape from the German clutches to the one place of Freedom in Europe — the British Isles — to fight on

To me there was the excitement of watching fighters engage in dogfights overhead, or the grand illusion of fireworks on display during the nightly air raids, of searchlights, of anti-aircraft guns, amid tracers lighting up the night sky. The whistling of falling bombs, to be followed by a big bang, and then the tinkling of broken glass, was a symphony that became part of our lives.

I had dug a shallow trench in the back garden, and this was armed with my machine gun — a garden rake mounted through the handle of a garden spade. I have often wondered how many German pilots realised how close they had been to being shot-down in flames.

There was a mobile anti-aircraft gun that would occasionally set up for the night in our quiet suburban avenue, and so disturb the tranquillity of the night, adding to our excitement, and to the annoyance of the neighbours who simply wanted to sleep.

Of weekend trips to Streatham Common to sail our model boats, while Dad flirted with the lady ATS crew who managed their Barrage Balloon. This was one of many such balloons around London, aimed at keeping the Nazi Dive Bombers high and stop them doing to us what they had previously done in Poland.

Many of the schools and children were evacuated, some just sent to quiet rural areas, but some farther afield, to Canada or even to Australia. My sister's school was evacuated to Eastbourne on the South Coast. When Eastbourne received one of the first air raids of the War, my father insisted she came home, just in time to share our nightly Anderson air-raid shelter routine. From that time on my parents decided that the family should stick together.

Schools were closed during the early part of the war, while the air-raid shelters were being built. The Teachers rose to the occasion and opened their homes to the children with two sessions — half the class in the morning with half after lunch. In those days classes had about 50 pupils per Teacher. Paper was in short supply at that time and I learnt my Tables and my Alphabet on slate.

When we eventually re-started school, we found that all the metal railings around the school had gone — to build tanks or ships or something for the war effort. We were regularly asked to collect pots and pans for the same purpose or participate in fund raising campaigns — like "Spitfire Week" or "Warship Week"

The shortage of paper is remembered in another way. During the war many suburban cinemas were converted for mass catering and renamed "Civic Restaurants" An adequate two course lunch could be obtained for six pennies. Every morning at school time mother would give me the six pennies for lunch.

However, the local Fish and Chip shop could supply a piece of fish and some chips for two pennies, so guess where we went for lunch. There was some problem being served, because "no paper — no service" was the rule, but to us kids this was not a problem — we simply had our lunches poured into our school caps. Maybe that's why I lost my hair at an early age.

The money saved was used for luxury purchases, buns and cakes or whatever was available. Sweets were on the ration, and the only chocolate that could be freely obtained was of the laxative type — the result was a natural disaster.

Clothing was severely rationed on a Points system, including shoes. Because children grow fast, it was legislated that if our feet measured more than nine inches we would obtain a special allocation of Points. I can remember being lined up for the measurement in our socks, and then wriggling my toes so that I would qualify with the required nine inches.

The Points system opened the door for the Black Marketeers. My sister, then 19 years old, was working for a car hire company, whose main clients were night club entertainers. Her boss who was into all the rackets decided to go to Cornwall to rest from the blitz, and we looked after their dog called Peter during this time. My sister would be given a car to pick up rare luxury foods from various Clubs, things such as we had not seen since the beginning of the war. Our family lived well during those weeks and the dog had to make do with cans of dog food.

One evening, during our mealtime, we heard the dog chewing on something beneath the table. On inspection, we found the ruins of mother's new shoes that she had used precious Points to Purchase. When told later of this disaster, the boss simply opened a drawer of his desk and gave my sister sheets of Points coupons for my mother to buy replacements. He made a lot of money during the war.

We were often late for school because of a hunt for pieces of air raid shrapnel which we traded later at school. This would also include a morbid interest in recent bomb sites — houses that had been destroyed by German bombs in the previous night's air raid.

Black cartridge paper and battens were given free to replace windows that were shattered by nearby bombs, while most people glued tape on their windows to avoid injury from flying fragments if this happened. Such precautions were taken also on public transport with heavy netting glued on the windows, but often scratched off by passengers.

The London Transport people created a defence against this vandalism by means of a cartoon character they named "Billy Brown of London Town" and they posted a poem on the walls of trams and buses that read:

"I hope you'll pardon this correction,

But that stuff's there for your protection "

Of course it did not take long for some wags to cross this message out, and replace it with –

"Thank you for this information

But I need to see my destination"

We very quickly learnt to tell the difference in engine noise between the more staccato noise of German planes and the smoothness of the British Rolls Royce Merlins. This was particularly useful on the occasions that the Germans would machine gun the streets, giving us time to shelter in shop doorways on the way home from school.

Later on, when the air-raid sirens sounded while we were at school, we would file into the shelters, to carry on our lessons or play games like "Mrs O'Grady says do this" or to sing Folk Songs or Sea Shanties. I can remember many of those songs to this day. Because the raids might be prolonged, we each had an emergency tin of iron rations, usually some rare bar of chocolate or fruit cake or such.

After a somewhat limited time in the Shelter, children would complain of intense starvation and Teacher would concede surrender by saying "OK open your ration tins" to be accompanied by shrieks of "Thank you, Hitler!" or "Good old Goering"

The daytime raids finished with the victory of the Battle of Britain, and were replaced by the routine nightly bombing of the Blitz. The Germans seemed very methodical in

2. My Wartime Boyhood and the Blitz on London

Lessons in the School Shelter

their approach by keeping to a schedule. We matched theirs with our own. Home from school about 4-30pm, an early meal about 5-30pm, and then after ablutions and a change into nightwear, we were packed into the Shelter for our homework and the inevitable game of Monopoly. Night after night after night this happened, until the Germans realised that they would never break our spirit this way and turned their attention to Russia.

It was about 1943 that the kerosene heater fell over and burnt out the contents of our Shelter. Very soon after, unusual rain caused flooding and the shelter became a swimming pool. For the rest of the war, when the bombing was more spasmodic, we just went to bed in the house and hoped.....

Later in the war, the Germans sent over the Flying Bombs — christened the Doodle Bugs- one of the first jet planes. These were unmanned, and would fly until the engine cut out and then they would crash. Each was loaded with a ton of explosive, and caused great damage. The greatest fear was that we never knew where they would land. Some would glide for ages without power, and some would crash immediately after the engine stopped. This period of silence had a tension of its own.

Nearly every anti-aircraft gun in the UK was moved South, and shot the majority down, or our Typhoons, the only fighter we had fast enough to catch them, would tip them over by the wing tips, upsetting their gyro controls and send them back to Germany. Those that got through did enormous damage, but by then most of us had become complacent about being under fire.

These Doodle Bugs — or V1's — were followed by the German V2 rockets which were really like being under shell fire. They were the forerunner of our Space Rockets and had the power to enter Space and then arrived at an astronomic speed, far greater than the speed of sound. If you heard the strange whoosh of their arrival, you knew you were safe. Their Nazi inventor, Professor Braun, was captured in 1945 and soon thereafter became the head of the U.S. Space Agency. This eventually led to the first Lunar landing by Apollo 11 in 1969.

My friends and I spent much of our holiday time on Box Hill in the North Downs near Dorking, and overlooking the main highway to the South Coast. We noticed the gradual build-up of tanks, guns, shells and other military hardware, being stored at the roadside for the eventual invasion of Europe.

I remember the excitement at school when the news of the allied landing at Normanby came to us — D Day at last, and then information about the gradual advance across Europe and finally the German collapse. Suddenly it was all over in Europe –VE Day (Victory in Europe) was celebrated by joining the crowds outside Buckingham Palace — a day of celebration to remember.

It was in this period that we saw newsreels of the Nazi concentration camps like Belsen, Buchanfeldt, etc, as they were occupied by the Allied armies. We learnt too the horror of the Death Camps, and the gas chambers built to slaughter millions of Jews. This was followed by the Nuremburg trials, where some of the Nazi leaders were tried for unbelievable war crimes. We were very cynical about German people who denied knowing what was happening to the Jews, with it going on right under their noses.

The war against Japan, so vital to the security of Australia, and fought across the Pacific Islands, and in Burma and S.E. Asia seemed part of another world, even though there were still many of our Forces involved. The conflict would go on for another six months after Germany surrendered, to be terminated by Japan also surrendering with the dropping of the first nuclear bombs on Hiroshima and Nagasaki.

That was the end of World War 2, but not to the end of fighting, which seems to have never stopped -continuing somewhere in the World. Politics and Religion would ensure that the Human Race would never find the hoped for Peace.

Post War Sequels

Many years later, and well after my father had died, my mother gave a dinner party. Among the guests was Paddy O'Reilly, who had been my father's Adjutant in both Palestine and the Home Guard. My mother became a little nostalgic and said to Paddy "You men were so wonderful, the way you would go down to the Headquarters to train those young fellows night after night all through the war years"

Paddy looked quite quizzical at first and then said "Did you know, Winifred, one of the best kept secrets of the War was that we only trained on Thursday evenings. The other evenings were spent at the local pub."

Songs of the Period — many made popular by Vera Lynn singing with the troops.
- White cliffs of Dover.
- Wish me luck, as you wave me goodbye.
- We'll meet again.
- Run Rabbit, run.
- Hang out the washing on the Siegfried Line.
- Roll out the Barrel.

A local post war Memory.

Early in my period at the Melbourne Maritime Museum, there occurred the death of the Japanese emperor Hirohito. At that time, many of the Volunteers who had contributed their time to the restoration of Polly Woodside had served in the war against Japan, and a few had been 'slaves' as POW's in building the infamous Thai railway.

At that time, the Australian authorities issued an order that this death should be commemorated by all national ensigns being flown at half-mast, and the National Trust followed suit.

As CEO I was approached by a delegation of Volunteers, and issued with the warning that if I complied with this order from Head Office, I would never see these volunteers again. I therefore decided that I would do the opposite, and organised that the ship would be 'dressed overall' as a mark of celebration, and to hell with any consequences.

(I chose to ignore the fact that most of the people concerned were driving Japanese cars and using Japanese products in their homes.)

3. The Post World War Two Period.

Having been born in the thirties, I was a product of a typical, middle class English boyhood between the wars, still with the belief in Empire and the British responsibility towards its subjects, with a sense perhaps of paternalism but certainly not of the equality of other races. This was fostered by the celebration of Empire Day. I was too young to be aware of the pressures of the Great Depression, and firmly believed in the heroes of past conquest, of discovery, and worldwide colonisation, back solidly by the strength of the Royal Navy and our control of the seas.

There was a feeling of continuity and invincibility, and for youngsters these attitudes were encouraged by reading the Boys Own Paper, Biggles, and a whole host of paper comics.

Christmas Day, with the Royal Address preceded by a world-wide hook-up around a British Commonwealth, "The Empire on which the Sun never sets", (all those pink bits on the map) only endorsed this emotion. From the backblocks of Bombay, to the noise of Hong Kong, and then the loneliness of the far-away people on a huge cattle station in

Australia, all this fostered the feeling of family, strength, and Britishness. The people of British descent, wherever they lived in the World, seemed part of one big family mainly sharing values and a way of life.

This attitude was fostered, indeed encouraged, by the middle-class public (**private** in other countries) schools. In fact, the introduction of sport in schools in the early 1840's began a whole new concept of education. The old saying (sometimes attributed to the Duke of Wellington) was that "Waterloo was won on the playing fields of Eton".

With its enforced support for school activities and sports teams, it's Army Junior Training Corps (which meant that participants would automatically go to Officer Training if enlisted) and with its total support for National institutions, such an attitude was inbred. Britain supported the concept of "the white man's burden" and had paternalistic attitudes towards other Races within the Empire. This attitude today would be labelled 'racist'.

We were brought up confident in all things British, and an exaggerated sense that we were different, compared with other peoples, a sort of chosen race. We were proud of our history, proud of our institutions, and scoffed at the politics of other countries. The people of Australia, New Zealand, Canada, and other 'white' Commonwealth countries were seen as extensions of our own country, and in fact there were not many people who did not have relatives living in these places, still referring to the U.K. as "home".

3. The Post World War Two Period.

Even on my first voyage to Australia in 1949 the anti-Pommy 'wharfies' referred to our ships as the "Home Boats".

For my generation, it was still considered normal to think of a future for ourselves beyond the shores of England, either in short term service or as a permanent settler. Those who entered the armed forces, the Colonial service, law enforcement, or our major trading companies, expected overseas postings to some far flung corner of the world as a normal course of events.

Every family had somebody living or serving overseas. These expectations took priority over any thoughts of home and family. The British Commonwealth and Empire were a worldwide operation and we were part of it. The British merchant ships were the glue that held it all together, under the protection of the Royal Navy.

Even after the end of WW2 in 1945 we had posters at school advertising careers in The Hong Kong or Palestinian Police, or in the Royal Indian Navy. My own brother served with the British Army in the Suez Canal Zone. It was inconceivable even then that the British Empire would collapse in so few years.

British people took their way of life, their attitudes, and their values with them where ever they went, so the world came to know that strange British character who never became completely localised where ever he was found, and never felt it necessary to adopt native customs. He had a reputation for being stand-offish. He took his sports with him, and founded cricket and rugby Clubs all over the world, with perhaps memories of some village green in Britain.

I saw an instance of this when staying on a tea plantation in the high country of Ceylon, now Sri Lanka. My host was a young unmarried British tea planter, the only European among thousands of Tamil workers, and who insisted on dressing for dinner every night, reading three week's old copies of the Times and who punctuated his life with a weekly drive to a Country Club many miles away, to mix with others of the same background. He only endured the presence of a young Cadet for three weeks because I had my Mess Kit uniform with me.

I visited the Club with him a couple of times. It was very a much version of our own Old Boys' Club back in England, and even after Independence, there were very few non-British members.

A personal example of this failure to adopt native ways is that although for five years I sailed with Chinese crews and learnt to enjoy Chinese food, even to this day I have never learnt to use chop sticks. Why should I. Civilized people have learnt to use a knife and fork.

For all the scorn that is held for these Colonials, they were trusted (or was it feared ?) by their workers. I witnessed a couple of occasions in Ceylon where there was a dispute in the workers' village, and settled by the Planter literally holding Court on his veranda, basing his judgements not on the Law, of which he knew little, but on the sense of fair play instilled in him during his early years at school in Britain, and accepted by the workers. Was this practical "paternalism" or was it based on power? I still believe that the attitude of "Play up and play the game" was the key.

Life under such a regime was not based on money — it was never mentioned at these levels. It was just assumed that by being brought up in this way, one would become a leader or boss in whatever career was chosen, and just rewards would follow. Those of us who enjoyed this upbringing were trained to believe that we were born to run things.

This sense of fairness, of duty first, and responsibility, of "playing the game", was a product of the British middle class way of life, fostered by their schools, and furthered by their involvement in sports and other activity which were a major part of their education. We went to school six days a week, and there was no rushing away when school work finished. If you were not playing yourself, it was compulsory to support your team. The team came first, and there was no thought of today's "family time" This attitude of team membership prevailed on the battle field, on the playing field, or in far flung outposts of Empire.

The worst thing an arrival on a foreign shore any British person could do was to "go native" i.e.to adopt the dress, the habits, and the culture of the local people. To do so would bring scorn from fellow countrymen. So many young people today will give up shaving, or wear a sarong, and fail to clean their shoes. There is a feeling perhaps in today's younger community that this lack of self-pride, of bad manners or such, is a sign of toughness. I remember the old saying -"manners maketh man". The main trouble seems to be that a poor example is set by the parents today.

There was also nothing like "counselling" as there is today. This was the era of the "stiff upper lip" and has led to a certain scornful attitude by elders to what is a huge industry today.

Post War Britain

Turning my thoughts to my last years at school after 1945, the war was over, the lights were on again, but although Britain had been the leader in standing up for freedom and democracy against the evil of Hitler and the Axis powers, it was broke — and all the previous wealth had gone. The Americans had the money, and made us crawl for it. After all, it was them that won the war with their huge resources, even if those of us in Britain could not bring ourselves to acknowledge that. The greatest thing the U.S. did in those post war years was Marshall Aid — pouring money into the ruins of Germany and Europe to avoid another war later, but Britain saw little of it and was literally held to ransom to rid itself of "enslaved" colonies.

Food rationing was worse than during the war, British factories were worn out, and suffered from many power shutdowns, and the Nation's whole logistical structure was crippled. Some say the situation was worsened by the Labour Government nationalising Road and Rail Transport and the Coal Industry, but they had to do something — thousands of young men had fought and died for a better, less classed, society. The greatest thing they did was to bring in the National Health Scheme, now still the envy of the world.

From the point of view of the average British citizen the granting of freedom and independence to those outposts of Empire really had little effect on their attitudes. The spirit of the Battle of Britain carried on and only endorsed the inborn belief in themselves, their heritage, and their position as a world power.

Probable the first real awareness of a changed situation was the flood of coloured people from the West Indies, West Africa, and India and Pakistan, in fact from all over the world wide Empire. Britain had boasted for years that all these people were British citizens, and now they were claiming their birthright.

The white working class felt dismayed when they unexpectedly had to share their hard-won welfare state with arriving waves of Bangladeshis, West Africans, and the rest, and this feeling continued for some years as waves of other coloured "British" citizens arrived. These people came from a different culture with a low standard of living and education and these differences became apparent as they became inhabitants of city suburbs, causing property prices to fall and unrest to increase.

I can see the much the same thing happening in Australia today, under the guise of a multi-cultural society, but really to supply a much needed work force. Time is a great healer and even a conservative old timer like I am has to acknowledge the benefits of multi-culturism.

By education and inter-mingling, Britain has become largely a multi-cultural nation, generations later, but older people still remember those days and those feelings, and the effects upon our attitudes.

As I have said before, these feelings are not so much based on colour of skin, but on a lingering feeling of paternalism. Perhaps we still felt superior, with a hangover of the "white mans' burden, but I challenge the word "racist". Perhaps a proportion of the Brexit vote was caused by this hangover — certainly free access to Britain by various migrants and refugees is still an issue.

Relationships throughout the Commonwealth

It was because of this influx that politicians felt something had to be done. Unfortunately, those in the Government at the time did not have the guts to admit that the predominately white countries of the Commonwealth, like Australia, New Zealand, etc; were members of the older far-flung family, and had supported the Home country in two World Wars.

3. The Post World War Two Period.

It should always be remembered that up to 1951 there was no such thing as an Australian passport, and Australians travelled as British subjects. I can understand the pride that young Australians have now in their country, but the talk about Australians fighting in 'other peoples' wars' shows me that there is little knowledge of History, and ignores the earlier feeling of belonging to a worldwide Family.

A general law for Visas to enter Britain was imposed. Naturally, Australia, for instance, retaliated with similar bans for non-Australian subjects, and the first of legal wedges was driven. Before I became an Australian citizen I was classed as a : "British Citizen — permanent resident of Australia" — and later this meant obtaining a Visa to come home every time I went overseas, which was pretty frequent at the time. I was already able to vote in Australian elections, and was in the Royal Australian Navy Reserve, and was proud to consider myself an Australian, but it was this silly Visa thing that was my main reason for becoming naturalised.

This situation worsened when Britain joined the European Union, and Australians were humiliated by having to queue at migration barriers with a hotchpotch of foreigners, while they saw Europeans going through without visas.

The Colombo Plan.

While America sponsored the generous Marshall Plan,

in 1948 the newly formed Commonwealth founded the Colombo Plan whereby students from the emerging nations were offered opportunities for learning and training at various Universities throughout the Commonwealth in the more developed Nations, with a view to returning to their home Nations and thus passing the knowledge on to the ultimate benefit of that country. It was a great success at that time.

Unfortunately, in recent years it has become a brain picking exercise and used as a way of solving the problem of skilled professional shortages, by using the now trained students as migrants and granting them permanent residence. This bastardised the whole concept, and particularly giving rise to corruption and all sorts of rorting. This criticism is perhaps magnified by perhaps the granting of Visas and Citizenship in Australia to those with sufficient money.

The Commonwealth of Nations

The Commonwealth itself has strangely expanded, and for democratic nations who rule by a Parliament and Law and Order, it is today a rival to the United Nations. From the original eleven nations in 1947, today its membership is over seventy nations, as witnessed by the Commonwealth Games recently. There are many Nations clamouring to join. The main difference today is that the prefix "British" has been dropped from the title, but member Nations must be "democratic" and all that entails to reach a necessary standard of membership.

Some nations who do not live up to the required standard of democracy have been expelled, such as South Africa because of Apartheid and Uganda under Idi Amin, who finally fled into exile in Saudi Arabia.

Britain is not the power that it was, nor has much influence in a world dominated by the Americans, and now threatened by the Chinese. However, I still believe in the British way of life, and the institutions of Justice and Democracy that go way back into history, in fact some say to the Magna Carta, and I sincerely hope that they will survive into the future of a changing and darkening world.

Some might say this condition only exists if you are white, but the facts of today's Commonwealth do not support this. Those of us lucky enough to be living under the British style of Law, take our freedom and rights for granted, but we must today be vigilant and to stand up for the values we believe in.

PART TWO

MY YEARS AT SEA.

4. Why I Chose the Merchant Navy

It was spring 1944. The Blitz was over, and only the odd bombing raid disturbed our nights. We had given up our nightly sojourns in the Anderson shelter, and Hitler was just starting his Doodle Bug campaign. The V2 rockets were yet to come.

We lived near London. Father was in charge of the local Home Guard, later renowned as TV's "Dad's Army". Mother was a Fire Watcher, rostered for duty with her steel helmet, stirrup pump, and bucket of sand.

I was 12 years old, and my elder brother John was 17. We were both students at a middle layer Public School. ("Private" in Australia). We both went to the Whitgift School which was steeped in history and tradition, being founded in 1593.

My brother was a great product of the system. He was a school prefect, Drum Major of the school JTC Cadet band, and he also played Rugby in the first fifteen. He was an ideal student, and won a Special Entry scholarship to the Royal Naval College, normally at Dartmouth, though it had then been evacuated to Chester in the North to avoid the bombing. He became what was called in the RN as a Midshipman, nicknamed as a 'Snottie' in professional terms.

The great day for him to start his new career arrived. We piled into Dad's car, and drove John to the London rail terminus. He was looking splendid in his brand new naval regalia — shining brass buttons and all.

At the station we bumped into a previous school mate of John's. He had left school early to start his cadetship at sea with the Blue Funnel Line. Nothing about him told of his occupation, except in the lapel of his tweed sports jacket was a small badge with the letters MN. (This was worn with pride by the civilian members of the Merchant Navy)

We learnt that he had just completed "Survivor's Leave", having been torpedoed in the North Atlantic, and was just off to Liverpool to join his next ship, and to probably to do it all over again.

The impression on me was extreme, and the contrast between my uniformed brother, and this real, young nondescript hero was just too much. To hell with the snob value of an RN Officer's life and an envious and secure career with the Royal Navy. It was the Merchant Navy for me.

This was to be not the only time in my life where I was guided by my heart and not more sensibly by my head. Looking back, there have been many such decisions in my life — a choice between wealth and career progress, or opportunity, and an emotional reaction. "There is a Tide in the affairs of men..." That's how Shakespeare saw life.

The lack of substantial personal wealth is perhaps the only evidence of the resultant outcome of the decisions I have made in my life. But then, how do we measure success?

Wealth is only money and I have little to show, but I am proud of the many things I have achieved over the years. I am now thankful for those decisions in past, and most of all for the basic lessons learnt during my years at sea which taught me the true value of life.

The day John joined the Royal Navy

5. Tramping the World

It was during this period between 1948 and 1953 that I coined the phrase: "The world is my playground." I was an Apprentice Deck Officer, aged from 16 to 20 years old, indentured with Saint Line, which was in essence a tramping company with no fixed run between ports. The ship would load for a foreign port, and on the way to that place the Managers would find another cargo for the next passage.

The length of trips and the time away from home really did not concern me. I loved the life at sea, although as apprentices we did all the dirty jobs. Unlike the other crew members we got no overtime payments. In fact in those days, as cadets our pay was negligible — from sixty pounds in the first year rising to an enormous sum of one hundred pounds (that's $200) in the fourth year. We even had to save money for the period ashore for our examinations, for there was no payment for Study Leave at that time, and we had to resort to the Dole, or Unemployment Benefit. In those days this payment was the enormous sum of $3.50 per week.

Soon after this, and for my subsequent examinations, we received full pay for three months Study Leave, with an additional one month's pay if we failed any one of the three parts of our exams. It became common practice to fail the Signals Examination, which was the easier part of the whole exam.

The shipping company had to undertake our training as future Desk Officers and Navigators, and the Merchant Navy Training Board sent us annual examinations by mail. Our Indentures were written many years before and were quite historic. I remember we signed that we would "not enter houses of ill repute." At sixteen, I probably had no idea what that even referred to. At least we were well fed, had no living expenses, and lived as officers aboard the ships, dressing in full uniform when not in working gear.

As far as I was concerned, all I cared about was that I was at sea, and being paid to see the World. How lucky was I.

6. The Leaving of Liverpool

My First Ship and my First Voyage

Liverpool, November 1948. Dull, drizzley, dirty, and tired from six years of war. Britain was generally in a condition of economic ruin. Food rationing was worse than at any stage of the war. Petrol was impossible to obtain privately, and power blackouts, with strikes and factory lockouts very common. The community was disillusioned -this was not the land of milk and honey they had been fighting for.

But for me the Sun was shining, and life was exciting.

Just ten days previously I had been selected as a Deck Officer Cadet with Saint Line. Instead of spending some months at pre-sea training college I was actually Outward Bound and in Liverpool to join my first ship — the "Saint Gregory" and starting my career as a member of Britain's then still great Merchant Navy.

I was sixteen and one month old, and had only just left an English Public School. Fair haired, fresh faced, and a little "plum in the mouth" would be an apt self-description.

Just ten days to get all my clobber together. New brass

bound uniforms, wet weather gear, (this was the old oil skins in those days.) and working gear — boiler suits and dungarees, (called jeans now) Nobody explained that really all we needed was plenty of working gear!

Nothing was going to dull this moment for me. Farewell to Mum and Dad at Euston in London -"You will not come to Liverpool — I'm a sailor now!" They were all steam trains in those days, and took about three hours to get from London to Liverpool. I should have known that I shared the train with many M.N. people and in later years I learnt to recognize the Navigators by their wooden sextant boxes, a badge of their profession.

Getting off the train at Lime Street Station, Liverpool, and then into a taxi. In my best command voice I ordered the driver: "Take me to the Saint Gregory at West Float, Birkenhead" and "OOh aye there la" was the typical Liverpudlian, and rather nasal sounding accent response I got.

(The Saint Gregory. — My First Ship).

The "Saint Gregory" (ex "Empire Heywood") was a WW2 built coal burning steam ship with a top speed of about eleven knots, and a typical cargo ship of that day. As the "Empire Heywood" she had seen service in Atlantic convoys during the Battle of the Atlantic during World War 2, and was present at the D-Day invasion of Europe.

After the war, she had been used by the British

6. The Leaving of Liverpool

Liverpool and River Mersey

Government to take illegal Jewish migrants from Israel to Cyprus, an operation described in the movie "Exodus". It was an effort by the British to honour an Agreement with the Palestine Arabs to partition the area of Palestine covered by the British Mandate, which had expired in 1948.

Because of this work, the ship was bombed and damaged in Haifa by Israeli terrorists in 1946, and after repairs in Gibraltar was sold to Saint Line of London and re-named "Saint Gregory."

The accommodation for the four Apprentices, known as the Half Deck, was a deck house located on the Boat Deck, and originally occupied by the Army gun crew carried by merchant ships during the war. These gunners were known as the DEMS, short for Defensively Armed Merchant Ships.

Sitting on the edge of my seat as the taxi sped towards

Birkenhead, I looked at the shipping on the River Mersey. Ships that traded all over the world, for Liverpool had long been one of the busiest seaports in Britain. Many of the ships were members of famous liner Companies, like Blue Funnel, NZS, Port Line, Blue Star, Cunard, Furness Withy, etc. and there were general cargo ships and tankers, busy little tugs, lighters and ferries. There was every thing I had ever dreamt about.

We drove through the Mersey Tunnel, and along cobbled streets, all shining and slippery with the drizzle. Then a sudden sharp left turn into a great barn of a cargo shed, piled high with grey stacks of bagged potatoes. The wet floor was littered with squashed spuds. The "Saint Gregory" was loading a full cargo of potatoes for Alexandria, in Egypt.

The taxi stopped alongside an open cargo door, through which I could see a sheet of rusty steel. I had arrived ! The

*The "Saint Gregory" (ex "Empire Heywood"),
a WW2 built coal burning steam ship*

6. The Leaving of Liverpool

driver helped me to the gangway with my gear, and this was quickly wizzed up on deck by two Chinese crew members.

I was met at the top of the gangway by the Second Officer, Mr. Hunter, who was unrecognizable in an oily boiler suit and beret. He was accompanied by an equally stained character, John Masson, who was the senior cadet, and who became a close friend and shipmate for the next two years. We are still in contact nearly seventy years later.

John was told off to help me stow my gear in the Cadet's quarters — the Half Deck — and then to take me to meet the Chief Officer, known on every ship as The Mate.

With some apprehension we entered the Officers' accommodation, paused at the paneled door and tapped gently. A gruff "enter" and I came face to face with the man who would be my boss, my teacher, my sea father, and my persecutor for most of the next four years.

"Butch" McKenzie was a typical product of the Merchant Navy. Starting his apprenticeship in the early 1930's, he battled through the Great Depression, which was really cruel to seamen. He was torpedoed three times during the war, and now was waiting for his first command.

This breed were real professional sailors. They were trained in the old ways, often by the last of the sailing ship men. Close enough was just not good enough, with pride in the job and in their ships — it did not matter whether it was an ocean greyhound or an indifferent tramp. Those of us who went to sea in the forties and fifties were in fact privileged to be trained by such men, but at the same time we enjoyed conditions that had only been dreamt of by them before the war.

"Where have you been? We were expecting you yesterday." I was too scared to answer. "Well it is 3-30, so no time for you to work on deck, so I want you to run an errand across the river for me."

"Go across to Liverpool, find this chemist, and pick up my prescription. Remember we sail at 8pm on the tide, so there's no time for shlly shallying around.

Down the gangway — my first shore leave! With a well chosen nautical gait, I made my way to the ferry terminal. Crossing the river on a crowded ferry, and being in uniform I was hoping I would not be sea sick.

In those latitudes, it is dark around 4pm in November, so through the gloom I tracked down the pharmacy and completed that part of my mission. Heading back to the ferry terminal I noticed it was getting foggy. By the time I was at the riverside, it was a real pea souper, and the air was full of fog signals, ranging from grunts to screams.

At the terminal there were loud speakers announcing the termination of services because of the fog. Desperation and despair! I clutched at the arm of an official and explained that I would be hung as a deserter or worse if I didn't get back to the ship on time.

The man looked at my brand new uniform — "Your first trip, Son? I nodded, almost in tears, "Well, he said, "there's

6. The Leaving of Liverpool

one ferry fitted with radar leaving soon for East Float, so at least you'll be on the right side of the river" He showed me the way aboard, and off we went into that thick yellow mucky pollution.

This was my first experience of thick fog at sea, always an erie experience, especially when one is surrounded by fog signals, and the difficulty of identifying where and how far away your closest neighbour.

Perhaps you have noticed that when a ferry arrives, within seconds all the passengers disappear into the night? This is what happened. Standing alone in a strange place and not able to see a hand in front of my face was scarey. I knew I had the river in front of me, and I knew I was East of where I needed to be.

Feeling very lonely and very desperate, I shuffled blindly along the cobbled streets, totally lost. The only company was the sound of shipping fog horns on the river. A voice inside me was telling me that my career was over before it had even started. Worse, the Mate, Mr. McKenzie, would not have his medicine.

A new sound! The rattle of a bicycle on the cobble stones, together with footsteps, and eventually the yellow glow of a lamp. I rushed up and almost in tears said "Can you help me please, I'm lost"

"Where are you going, lad?"

"My ship, the Saint Gregory, is at West Float, and is due to sail about now."

"Not in this fog she won't. Anyway, come with me, I'm due down there to let her lines go, whenever she can go."

And that is how I started my first voyage and my seagoing career.

Epilogue –and how I got my nickname.

The fog lifted enough for us to sail at about 9pm. I was appointed Cadet to the Middle Watch (12 to 4) with the Second Officer. Just before midnight, the Third Officer send his Cadet down to the Half Deck with the words " You had better go and wake up the Cherub " It took some years of hard living to shake off that nick-name ! Years later, I still get a Christmas Card from John (that Cadet) addressed to "The Cherub".

I will always remember my first Watch at sea. It was crystal clear and icy, with a flat calm sea reflecting the stars, as we gently rolled westward into the Irish Sea. The very last of the fog cleared away ahead of us, and to my surprise there was revealed this large and glittering body, just fine on the starboard bow.

I went into the wheelhouse and reported "Object nearly right ahead; it looks like an ice-berg "

"Very good — carry on" was the Second Mate's response to my report — very coolly, I thought.

Sometime later I was very agitated. The object ahead had disappeared. I went back into the wheelhouse to say that

I could no longer see it. The Second Officer (very gently) laughed. "I guess you have never seen the Moon setting down into the sea horizon before. "

He was kind enough not to make it a humiliating story at breakfast in the Saloon later that morning.

7. My first foreign seaport — Alexandria in Egypt

The ship had arrived mid-morning at the historic, almost pre-historic, seaport of Alexandria. The home of the long-gone lighthouse and the famous library destroyed by fire, centuries ago. It was known as the "Seaport of the Pharaohs". I was enthralled.

The mass of humanity on the shore, the warm air, tempered with the strange smells, the blue Mediterranean Sea, the glaring white buildings, the sculpture of King Farouk's Palace, the Arab labourers in their baggy black trousers and their red fezzes. I am glad I saw all this then, because it has all gone now.

There were noises and action I had never heard before. The chanting of the dock workers, the rattle of the steam winches, the clang of cargo hooks bouncing against the steel hatch coamings, the bundles of sacks swinging from the cargo holds and downwards to be landed on the dock. Then the sacks dumped without ceremony on to the bare shoulders of the labourers to be carried in an endless stream of staggering humanity, snaking into the cargo shed, helped by the occasional thwack of a cane if that person was not showing enough enthusiasm.

This was a scene that I had pictured from book and movies — the old colonial world of the "white man's burden ". I am glad I saw it: like all good imperialistic British boys, I had been fed a diet of Biggles and Kipling. It has all gone now. Today, clothes are the same everywhere, and every foreign place is dominated by Coca Cola and McDonalds.

We four Cadets had been paired off to work with the Officer in charge of the deck, adjusting the ship's gear, and keeping an eye on the wharf labour, who would get up to all sorts of tricks and try to steal any gear lying around. They would even cut lengths of rope from derrick guys and mooring lines, or rob anything from the crew's quarters.

This first day my watch finished at 6pm, and I would not be back on deck until 10pm. (We worked 4 hours on and four hours off, while the dock workers worked about 20 hours a day) It was time to have a bite.

However, there were two brand new Egyptian merchant ships berthed astern of us, and fine looking vessels they were too. I can even remember their Names — "Star of Suez" and "Star of Aswan". I decided to make the most of the last of the sunshine and photograph these fine ships before I had my evening meal. So armed with my little box Brownie camera, I went down the gangway and on to Egyptian soil, my very first footsteps on a foreign shore.

Snap. Snap....and then "Ow!' I felt a sharp object butting

7. My first foreign seaport— Alexandria in Egypt

my ribs, and looking round here was this scruffy, really scruffy, and unshaven Egyptian soldier menacing me with his rifle. He gestured for my camera and then prodded me to walk towards a structure with armed sentries and the Egyptian flag flying above. This turned out to be a military defence base.

After much gibberish and pushing, I was ushered into the presence of an officer. It was dark by now, and the only light in that room was a desk light with a green shade. He pretended not to notice me and kept reading from a paper on his desk, while I stood nervously before him, with armed soldiers at the door behind me.

Eventually, he looked up, stared at me, and then told me that I would be charged as an Israeli spy.

Afterwards, it struck me how ridiculous this was. Me — the "Cherub" — a sixteen year old, blonde, pink faced English schoolboy, looking more like a Canterbury Cathedral choir boy than a threat to the Egyptian nation. At that moment I was too scared to think it funny and I felt very alone.

But of course, this was December 1948. The State of Israel has been declared a few months before and was at war with the surrounding Arab nations. There was also an irony about being accused of being an Israeli spy. At that time, I despised the Israelis. Earlier that year, the Israeli terror gangs had murdered British soldiers, and had even earlier blown a hole in my ship to stop her being used to transport Jewish illegal migrants back to Cyprus.

The Egyptian officer spoke: "Who are you — where are your papers". At least he spoke English. I tried to explain that I had only come ashore for a minute to take photographs, and never considered it necessary to have my British Seaman's I.D. card in my pocket. He didn't find that convincing, and my pleas for him to send for an Officer from the ship to identify me fell on his unlistening ears.

He told me that I would be locked up, and my camera film developed to see what secret defence facilities I had photographed. He then ordered me to strip to my under pants and be searched. This process became humiliating when he delved, probably with some pleasure, into the recesses of my anatomy. I felt like a latter day Lawrence of Arabia. I was then allowed to dress, and taken to a grubby cell, with no facilities and stinking of urine and worse. There was a sole wooden bench to sit on.

My wrist watch had disappeared during the search process and this was never returned, but at about midnight the door swung open, and an armed soldier beckoned me outside. I was escorted to an army truck, pushed aboard, and off we drove. I was terrified, and there was no explanation or English word spoken.

Our destination was another military facility. Soldiers were everywhere, barbed wire enclosures, and sand-bagged gun positions. Brought up on a diet of war films during the 1939 -1945 school years, I thought it all looked very familiar and very frightening. I was taken to a large office, told to be

7. My first foreign seaport— Alexandria in Egypt

seated, and I had to wait a long time with an armed soldier scowling at me throughout.

Finally, the door opened and in came an officer. The red tabs on his lapels indicated he had some rank.

"We have developed the film in your camera "were his first words in very good English. "Who asked you to photograph the harbour defences?"

"No. NO." I insisted. "I was just photographing those two lovely new cargo ships. "

"So you didn't intend that the gun placements on the breakwater would be also pictured?"

"I didn't even notice them" I said. He fixed me with a frozen gaze.

"Then where did you photograph those military aircraft"

The memory struck me like a sixteen stone Rugby fullback. The earlier part of that camera film had been used at an airshow some months earlier at a RAF base in southern England, and I had photographed various British and U.S. aircraft.

I tried to explain, but my host shrugged his shoulders and obviously did not believe me. He told me that I would be interrogated further by military Intelligence Officers — visions of Gestapo in black leather coats flashed through my brain.

I was escorted to a cell, given a cup of water from a chipped enamel tin mug and the door shut with a loud clang and the bolt rattled home. This was not funny ! I was a scared little boy and certainly not the tough young sailor that I had pictured myself to be only a few hours before.

Through a small window I could see the greying dawn. The door opened. I was ushered down the corridor back into the senior officer's office.

I cannot tell the surge of joy and relief when I saw that the ship's Third Officer was also in the room, with a cup of tea in his hand. John Hume was a Scot, the son of a tough Glasgow policeman.

"Ah there you are laddie", he said. "We have been a wee bit worried about you, but here you are, well looked after and safe and sound !" (In all the years I spent sailing with John this was the only time I witnessed the slightest diplomacy from him — hit first and talk later was the Glasgow method.)

I wanted to hug him, but that would not have been very British.

I learnt later that when I was found to be missing, the ship's Officers split up into search parties — some taking the opportunity to investigate the shadier parts of town. There was a rule in the Merchant Navy — you can lose anybody else, but don't lose an indentured Cadet. John had gone to the Military Post where I was first taken, to make inquiries, and then obtained my I.D. papers from my cabin. In any case, he was not a man to be trifled with.

The Egyptian Officer was transformed into a benevolent, paternal figure.

"I am so sorry for this misunderstanding. We are at war, and we can't be too careful. Hope you hold no grudges "

Before I could say a word, John interposed — "Well come along — breakfast is waiting on the ship, and this gentleman has kindly arranged transport for us."

The Army truck dropped us at the gangway, with the crew all lining the rails. I looked up, and the Captain and the Chief Officer were sternly gazing down from the wing of the Bridge.

The Senior Cadet came to me "Thank God you are safe" he said, followed by "The Mate wants to see you"

Epilogue.

This whole incident did not endear me to the Egyptian people, nor to Arabs as a Race. This was in contrast to the praise my father had heaped upon the Arabs, based on his experiences of living and fighting against the Turks while with the Bedouin Revolt raised by Lawrence. (He was seconded to Arabia after being wounded at Gallipoli)

After this first voyage, I can remember taking issue with him on this subject. His response — "Charles, you haven't met the true Arabs — and don't judge them all by that bumboat breed you met at Alexandria and in the Canal Zone."

It was many years later, and well after Dad had died, that I was working in Amman, Jordan, for the United Nations as a commercial consultant. We were there to find ways to create a viable economy for Jordan, in what was left of their country after the Israeli occupation of the sustainable area on the Western Bank of the Jordan River.

At that time, I had three Arab graduates working in my team, and I reported to the King's brother. From them all I received friendship and hospitality, and though their culture and their attitudes differed in many ways from my own, I came to learn respect, even humility, for their code and customs. The only difference I found was that they made a point of keeping the female members of the family out of sight, even when we were invited to their homes.

Their Arab culture was a lesson I would never forget, and gave me a new perspective to the situation throughout the Middle East. It was a stark contrast to the arrogance we experienced on our visits to Israel. But then the cabin boy always kicks the ship's cat when he's had a bad time!

I have always wished that I had learnt that lesson before the death of my Father, and thus the opportunity to say "Now I know what you meant."

8. Alexandria to Marseilles (Christmas — 1948)

The last of the cargo was ashore, and the hordes of Egyptian dock workers left the ship. The hatch beams were shipped, and the hatches battened down for sea. The lowering of the derricks and the squaring away of the cargo runners and gear was the next step, and once the sea pilot was aboard the accommodation ladder was raised and stowed.

One of the pre-sailing duties for we cadets was to re-rig the wireless aerials, and also the whistle lanyard that ran

Cadets washing down.

from the bridge to the shining brass siren on the funnel. These were always unshipped to keep the way clear for working cargo at number three hatch.

It was a few days before Christmas 1948, and we were under orders to sail for Marseilles on the south coast of France. The trip was to be "light ship" that is without cargo, and we relied on water ballast for stability. At our maximum speed of around ten knots, it was estimated that the trip would take seven days.

This was only my second departure from a port, so the routine was novel and exciting. The search for stowaways, the testing of the Engine Room Telegraphs and the blast on the whistle as the Third Mate checked the bridge gear, and finally the order " Stations for Leaving Harbour" saw me on the Foc'sle Head with the Chief Officer, the Carpenter on the windlass, and several of our crew. "Let go Forward " and " All clear Aft" and with the wheezing and vibration of the main engines, we were on our way.

A brief stop to drop the pilot who waved us farewell from his launch, and then the usual routine of tossing the rubbish into Davy Jones Locker (no worries about environment in those days) and washing the dirt of Alexandria away with sea water hoses.

We were on our way, and quickly settled down into the sea going routine. I was posted to the Eight to Twelve Watch with the Third Mate, whose main interest in life were the fortunes of the Sunderland soccer Team.

8. Alexandria to Marseilles (Christmas — 1948)

Our watches were four hours on, and eight off. We cadets would do sailor's work on deck during the daylight watch and be on the Bridge at night.

Sailors think about 'Trips' rather than days or weeks. Time at sea on a freighter becomes a routine round of watch keeping, sleeping, playing cards or chess, and days merge into nothingness. Whether it takes two days or six weeks between ports, it is a 'trip'

So there we were, steaming through perfect, tourist brochure Mediterranean weather — blue skies, gentle winds, and kindly seas. As a cadet, my income was pretty minimal, but to me, I was one of the chosen few, enjoying for free what others paid dearly for.

It would have been the fourth day of this trip, and it was Christmas Day. With no deck work to be done, I went up the Bridge at 8am to go on watch. What a sight greeted me! We were in the middle of the Straits of Messina, the narrow strip of water that separates Sicily from mainland Italy. On either side we could hear church bells ringing in the Christmas morn, and we could see people thronging the streets, perhaps rushing to church.

It was a picture book scene that has stayed with me down the years. My first Christmas away from home, my first at sea, and I still talk about it. And then — the crowning moment. We cleared the Straits, and as eight bells were made, and my watch was finished at mid-day, we were off the volcanic island of Stromboli. When the gong went to summon us all for Christmas lunch, Stromboli obliged with a puff of smoke, as if to say "Good Luck and Merry Christmas."

9. The Christmas Storm

It must have been that afternoon when we were somewhere towards Corsica. that I was summoned to the Bridge,

"Did you learn French at school ? " — a question from the Captain.

Answering in the affirmative, I was handed a Radio Message — "See if you can translate that for me"

I scurried back to the cadets' Half Deck, thrilled to be entrusted with this assignment and determined to make a job of it. The message was in French but nothing like the French I had learnt at school.

So engrossed with the task, I failed to notice that dark clouds had blotted out the Sun, that a rising wind was starting to sing through the rigging, and the ship was starting to pitch and roll.

I finished the translation, more or less, and rushed back to the bridge. This meant traversing the open deck between the funnel area and the bridge superstructure. As the ship rolled, my path was a zig zag of balance, and I was doused by a full dollop of spray breaking aboard.

Breathlessly and wet, I handed the soggy translation to the Captain. "It looks like a gale warning, Sir." It was indeed. It was a warning of a strong Mistral, the wind that blows down the Rhone Valley from the North, and very soon it was shrieking at something like fifty or sixty knots.

The Mistral, is one of several local winds that rise suddenly in the Mediterranean, and can catch many an unwary sailor napping.

Our ship was typical of the many mass produced ships built during the Second World War. Coal burning, with low power provided by a steam triple expansion engine, and capable of a maximum speed of under eleven knots. The American "Liberty" ships and the Canadian "Fort" types were similar, except these pioneered welded hulls. The British types were riveted and known as " Empire Ships" and the Saint Gregory had been built in Dundee in 1942 as the "Empire Heywood."

She had survived Atlantic convoys, worked as a supply ship for D Day at Normandy, and became one of those ships transporting illegal migrants from Haifa in Israel to Cyprus when the British were trying to honour their commitment to the Palestinians. This part of her career was short lived when the Jewish terrorists blew a hole in her bow at Haifa.

In her light ship condition, she was now no match for that powerful Mistral. She was a devil to steer, and each time the bow went down into a trough, the propeller would race,

9. The Christmas Storm

spinning as it came out of the water. The vibration felt like the ship would shake herself to pieces.

We were going nowhere, except downwind with massive leeway, and I heard the Captain say that if this continued, we would find ourselves ashore on the north coast of Africa. Something had to be done. We had to get the propeller biting into the water and regain control.

These typical five hatch ships of that vintage had the engine and boiler rooms amidships with the propeller shaft connecting the main engines to the propeller by running through a shaft tunnel built into Numbers Four and Five lower holds. This tunnel was about 10 feet high, and separated those lower holds into halves. Below the lower holds were the double bottom water ballast tanks, named Port and Starboard tanks, and now full of ballast water.

It was decided to flood these lower holds to a depth of about six feet, and by thus adding considerable weight changing the trim of the ship and putting the propeller deeper into the water.

It was a task for all hands. First of all the lower hold had to be cleared of anything stored there. This was mainly dunnage timber, used in stowing our last cargo. All of timber had to be lifted to the 'tween decks above, and this was done by hand because there was no way we could open the hatches in that weather to use the winches.

Once a section had been cleared, I was told off to work with the Carpenter. We had to unbolt the tank manhole covers enough to insert one inch timber wedges, and then tighten down the holding bolts again to hold these wedges in place, leaving a gap for water to enter. There were three man hole covers at each side of the tunnel in both holds. This means we had to open up twelve tank covers in all.

Remember all this was done while the ship was rolling perhaps 40 degrees or more, and pounding heavily from time to time. We were working by torch light in the bowels of the ship, and the noise of the ship working, creaking, and cracking and groaning was like being surrounded by dragons. Remember too — this was my first trip, I was sixteen — and I was scared! At least I was not seasick, and never have been. I just wished I was somewhere else!

As we finished each section, the engineers would open valves and gradually these lower holds were flooded. There is no doubt it saved the ship, and we started to make headway against the gale. But have you ever carried a basin of water. The water swishes from side to side — this is called "free surface effect" — and now this was added to our discomfort.

The ship would roll to one side, but instead of recovering, the unimpeded water would rush to that low side, and add a further few degrees to the roll. Then she would roll to the other side and the whole drama would be repeated. There were many times that I thought the ship would capsize!

We endured this for about eighteen hours, and then the gale gradually weakened, good headway was restored, and the engineers were able to start pumping out the lower holds so that loading could commence when we arrived at Marseilles. What a nice job for the Cadets! If we had visions of romancing French popsies, that had to wait. It was sawdust and sweeping and more sawdust and more sweeping until the holds were dry and loading could commence.

It was after all, to say the least, just an event in my career as a seafarer.

Loading truck at Marseilles

10. Marseilles to Saigon

I have already told in earlier chapters of the first voyages from Liverpool to Alexandria and thence Marseilles. Now, in March 1949, we were bound for Saigon in Indo-China (now Vietnam) loaded with supplies for the French Army.

The French were fighting to regain control of the French colony, following the defeat of Japan. They had sacked the Vichy people appointed by the Japanese invaders in 1940, but were struggling against the Vietnamese people who were fighting for independence. The French army at this stage was constituted mainly by Foreign Legionnaires, the majority of whom, we discovered, were young Germans unable to find other work in a Europe still devastated from WW2.

Our voyage from France to Saigon took us across the Mediterranean, through the Suez Canal, down the Red Sea to Aden, and then the long leg across the Indian Ocean to Singapore and thence Saigon. We took on coal bunkers in Port Said, Aden and Singapore, and therefore I was able to see the value of the coaling stations that had been the lifeline of the old British Empire, and when the majority of ships used coal.

To provide for the fuel and water for the long leg from Aden to Singapore, the Chinese crew were restricted to one bucket of water per day for each man and taken from the hand galley pump. The European officers and apprentices were not water restricted, but were honour bound to keep their usage minimal. Extra coal fuel was also piled on deck, for later transfer to the coal holds, which were known as the Bunkers, as space became available..

It was on this voyage that I learnt that sailors talk about "trips", whether a trip took a few days or many weeks. The routine at sea, with watch keeping on the bridge or in the engine room, just went on regardless and the time spent between ports became meaningless, unless some event, such as bad weather, a fire, or other emergency became a highlight. It was the time spent in Port that became the main memory and created perhaps a sailor's judgement of the place, even of the country and its people, in the sailor's eyes.

Swimming the Suez Canal

For me the highlight of this trip, with everything so new and strange to me, was the transit of the Suez Canal, being the first time that I saw it and its operations.

We arrived at Port Said early in the morning, and anchored among the ships assembled to head south in the next Southbound convoy. Whilst anchored, we loaded the

Canal searchlight with was hoisted by the special davit fitted in every ship and carried at their bow. The canal buoys at that time were simply reflectors and needed the searchlight to show the channel to the Pilot of each ship. We also loaded the two mooring boats that would take our lines to the shore when we tied up to the bank.

At this time there was no canal by-pass, and ships had nowhere to pass each other while underway. Consequently, the ships heading southward would tie up to allow the priority Northbound ships to have free passage. Because the depth of the Canal was limited, the "suction" of each passing ship was such that every ship tied up would need to absorb the "drag" by having their crew on mooring stations to constantly adjust their moorings.

Now a little background. Before going to sea, I was a fan for the books of an author named Percy. F. Westerman, who wrote stories about the adventures of Merchant Navy cadets. In one of his yarns, he described how two lads had swum across the Suez Canal so that they could boast that they had swum from Asia to Africa. His story may have been true or it may have been fiction, but it stuck in my memory, and I resolved that I would re-enact the act described.

At this time in 1948 the Canal Zone was garrisoned by thousands of British troops, the Canal being vital to the security of the remaining British Empire. They were there until the Egyptian independence of 1954. Also aboard the Saint Gregory was a scruffy mongrel dog named Susie, who was marooned aboard the ship by international quarantine laws, and who had made her home in the Half Deck. She slept in my cabin and as you will see, was very protective.

While at anchor in Port Said, we were besieged by the Egyptian traders in their "Bumboats" These men were treated by generations of British sailors as the lowest of the low, and were the participants in many two way swindles. A good example was the trading by one of our cadets of a box of Woodbine cigarettes for a bottle of Scotch Whiskey. It turned out to be a double swindle — the box of cigarettes was simply full of sawdust, and the bottle of Scotch was simply cold tea.

Me and ship's dog — Susie

I still possess a pair of brass pots that I purchased at Port Said on my first trip in 1948 as presents for my mother, and which she sent back to me before she died.

I can remember remarking about these traders to my Father, During WW1, he was in the Middlesex Yeomanry, and after being awarded and wounded with the British Army at Gallipoli, he had been sent to Arabia in support of the famous Lawrence.

He was very respectful of the Bedouin Arabs, and countered my comments by saying that we should not judge Arabs by the "Bumboat Men of the Canal, and to "just wait till you meet the real Arab people." It was many years later, after his death, when I was working with three delightful Arab economists in Amman, that I realised that what he said was so true. I would guess that the Bum Boats are now part of history, for it is many years since I last passed that way.

We sailed South about midday and then tied up to allow North Bound ships to pass at about three in the afternoon. One of the other apprentices and I quietly lowered a Pilot Ladder over the side, and began our swim to the other Egyptian side of the Canal, ignoring shouts from the ship to return. It was not far, about four hundred meters to the other bank, and we sat there for a while regaining our breath.

Suddenly, we were faced by an Egyptian soldier pointing his rifle at us and gesturing that he was taking us prisoner, presumably as "illegal immigrants". This was a bit frightening, and while we were pondering what we should do, we heard the screech of brakes, and a jeep loaded with Scots Guards pulled up. I can still hear that Scottish voice telling us to get back to our ship, and while half way back, we heard two splashes. One was caused by the rifle, and the other by the Egyptian soldier himself, unceremoniously dunked by the British soldiers.

This should have been the end of this historic event, but half way across the Canal we were met by Susie the dog, who was quite sure that we needed her help. This would have been lovely, but retrieving a heavy, waterlogged dog up a ship's side was a problem, only achieved by brute strength, and even worse than the roasting we received afterwards from the Chief Officer.

Still, we had done it! We had swum from Asia to Africa, a feat that would be impossible today because of the changes and duplication of that part of the Canal itself.

The South West Monsoon.

The other event I remember on this trip was my introduction to the weather of the Indian Ocean. After leaving Aden and the lee of Socotra Island, a steady South West sea and swell are encountered and made worse by the S.W. Monsoon, a seasonal wind that blows from June to September each year. It was by using this wind that early Arab traders fund their way from Africa to Asia, to be also followed by European sailors later.

Included in the cargo for Saigon was a long rail car, stowed on deck on the windward side of Number Four Hatch, and lashed down with wire straps. As we felt the full force of the monsoon winds, the ship started rolling quite heavily, and this railcar started to slide from side to side, threatening to break loose and cause damage to itself and to the ship. This was a job for the Apprentices — the Chinese sailors would not do it.

Under the supervision of the Chief Officer we started work, and I was told to go inside the railcar, and pass new lashings. This was pretty frightening, with the vehicle sliding from side to side, and when the ship rolled to starboard, I would be looking down into the sea, only a few feet below. I was certainly pleased when the job was done.

At Singapore we anchored in the Roads, signed on a new crew, and topped up with more coal bunkers. I had not realised before that our Chinese crew were almost like foreigners to each other. Our deckhands came from Shanghai, the engine room gang came from Canton and the catering staff from Hainan. They all spoke different dialects of Chinese, and had trouble communicating with each other. (This was one problem later solved by the Communist Government in China by adopting nationally the Mandarin language.) My earliest memory of the Chinese crew was the noise of the slapping down of Majong tiles being played in their mess room.

The Snake on the Monkey Island

It was on the afternoon after leaving Singapore that I was working on the Poop auxiliary steering gear, while the ship was steaming through the Malacca Straits. I was on the 12 to 4 Watch with the Second Officer, working on deck during the daylight hours and keeping Watch on the bridge at night. During the day, the Officer on the bridge would summon us by using a whistle if he needed us.

On this hot and steamy afternoon, I noticed a bird, some sort of hawk, passing over the ship, and when it was over the bridge I saw an object drop from its mouth. It proved to be a snake, about 25 Centre metres long.

Inevitably I heard a whistle blast and on reporting to the bridge was told that "There's a snake on the Monkey Island — fix it" Now, I also shared a fear of snakes with that Second Mate, but he was the boss and I had to obey.

In those days ships had both Fire Buckets and Rocket Sticks on each side of the Wheelhouse, so using two rocket sticks in a chop-stick system I picked up the stunned snake and deposited it into a fire-bucket. Very carefully I took this unwelcome load down to the main deck, and left it alongside Number Three Hatch for all to see.

A couple of hours later, on my way to the Saloon for our evening meal, I was shocked to see an empty bucket. There was immediate panic among the European officers — sailors are not used to snakes. That night, in spite of the heat and humidity, cabin doors were shut and ports battened down. Watch keepers on the bridge kept torches in their hands and the slightest sound would send shivers down each spine.

At six in next morning, when the Bosun reported to the Chief Officer for his orders for the day, he was told that the first priority was to "Find that damned snake"

The Chinese Bosun was puzzled. In his pigeon English he said "You mean snakee in bucket on main desk before chow? Me see before. Me no likee snakee. Me put overside before chow last night"

Thus ends this story of the great bravery shown by British sailors in the face of a small snake.

Arrival at Saigon

The city of Saigon lies some distance up the Saigon River from the sea. We passed upstream, past rice fields and rain forests, and came under a small level of rifle fire at one stage. The only evidence of this was a couple of bullet holes in the funnel.

The city itself was a mixture of French and Asian architecture, and was known in those days as the Beirut of the East. As a young man, my greatest memory was of the attractive Annamite girls in their long white dresses and conical hats.

Because of the emergency, a curfew was in place, and we were forced back to our ship by 10pm each evening. Many of the crew found it "necessary" to find a bed in the City itself. The heat and humidity were unbearable. Canvas awnings were rigged over the accommodation areas, and the Chief Officer thought it a good idea to hose down these regularly. This was a mistake, and thus these awnings became a breeding ground for legions of hungry blood sucking mosquitos, with a personal sequel of septic mosquito bites that led to hospitalisation later in Colombo.

We were invited to join in French army mess rooms, and to mix freely with the Foreign Legionnaires, who were mainly younger Germans, unable to gain work in their homeland. Their company and hospitality was great, and although I was still only sixteen years old, I enjoyed our stay.

It makes me sad to think that many of those young men would have been killed in the final battles with the Viet Cong. The history of the U.S. involvement and their fear of the Domino Effect of communism that led to partition between North and South, and the final defeat of the South is now history but is not part of this story.

Discharge of Cargo — Tragedy and a Pleasant Surprise.

It was during the discharge of the military cargo in Saigon that I was witness to my first experience with Death. It occurred in the Number Four Lower Hold, while I was working. One of the French supervisors was checking on the lifting of a heavy truck, when the slings gave way and he was killed instantly under the weight. I took part in the retrieval of his body, and this whole episode was a great shock to me.

This experience was repeated throughout my life but this was the initial shock. These days we would have been swamped by hordes of counsellors, but then we had to cope with it all ourselves, and I have since maintained a contempt for the softness of modern western life. Am I a worse person because of this this neglect? I really don't think so, but then I am from a "stiff upper lip" generation.

On a more pleasant note was an amazing and pleasant discovery. One of the jobs done by the Cadets prior to sailing was the re-rigging of the radio aerials and the whistle lanyard, both of which stretched across the gap between the bridge and the funnel, traversing Number Three Hatch.

It was while climbing up the signal mast above the Monkey Island to do this that I noticed a case of wine lying in the Bridge awning. It had fallen out of a cargo sling lifted from Number Three Hold, unseen or ignored by the crane driver, and it had been originally destined for the army's Officers' Mess.

I alerted the Radio Officer, whose cabin was just abaft the wheelhouse, and together we smuggled this loot into his cabin, for later enjoyment once we had sailed from Saigon. It turned out to be a beautiful and smooth French dinner wine and which was gratefully enjoyed at the "happy hours" spent each evening before dinner on the way to our next loading port — Bangkok in Thailand.

It was a tranquil and a pleasant voyage, with smooth seas and gentle winds, and thus a fitting introduction to the Orient, made even more pleasant by the cooling glass of the unexpected wine.

11. Loading rice in Bangkok

Our purpose in Bangkok was to load rice for Colombo in Ceylon (Sri Lanka). It was interesting, as we proceeded up the river, to see the Temples, and Palaces the floating communities, and the antiquated warships. The river is quite shallow, and did not allow deep draught vessels to load more than about a quarter of their full cargo, before proceeding out to an anchorage among the islands known as Goh Sichang.

It is customary for ships when visiting a foreign port to fly that country's National Flag, known to sailors as the Courtesy Ensign. On arrival in Thailand, we found that we did not have a Thai flag in our locker. This was solved by flying the "C" flag — the colours are actually reversed, but nobody noticed.

Rice is a tricky cargo to carry. It will generate vast quantities of water vapour which if allowed to remain, will condense into water, and cause the rice to swell. Ships have been known to literally burst themselves apart by this action. To avoid this happening, the cargo is stowed with a network of vents to carry the vapour away safely. The

Cadets were detailed to help the Officers ensure this system was undertaken. Because the labourers (they were referred to as "coolies" in those days) worked about 20 hours per day, the Officers, and Cadets were detailed into watches round the clock, and so were kept busy, with five cargo holds to keep a check on.

Because of the long hours of work, the wharf labourers lived aboard the ship, both in the city and later at the off-shore anchorage. A kitchen was set up on deck with female cooks, and a small shop was also set up to sell cigarettes and other bits and pieces that the men might require.

After loading for about three days in the City, we shifted to the island anchorage, and the bagged cargo was brought out to the ship in lighters. It was really a delightful and peaceful scene, especially when those of us off-watch were able to take a ship's boat ashore to a beautiful island beach for swimming parties. In subsequent voyages to Bangkok we learnt that some Norwegian sailors were devoured by sharks at that very same spot. This put paid to our similar pleasures.

After we sailed, the mosquito bites suffered in Saigon had become very infected. My legs and ankles were swollen, giving me problems in walking. I was taken off work and forced to rest, and on arrival in Colombo I was immediately transferred to a hospital for treatment.

12. Ceylon (Sri Lanka) 1950

The infection in my legs, which put me into hospital in Colombo, was really a golden goose for the local doctors, who now contended that my heart had been affected. My hospitalisation was extended even after the ship sailed for Calcutta, and it was decided that I should be sent out of the heat of Colombo to a cooler climate and to a tea plantation in the cooler hill country.

As a result I spent three weeks at a place called Maskalia, staying with a young British planter whose only condition for having me as a guest was that I had my evening Mess Kit with me.

Before leaving the hospital for the hills, two of the nurses to whom I had previously admitted that I had an obsessive fear of snakes, told me all sorts of stories about the precautions I should take when on the plantation. Things like inspecting the underside of a dining table and banging my chair hard on the floor before sitting down.

When I had my first meal there I went through this routine to the amazement of my host, who asked what the hell I was doing. I explained, only to be told that there were no dangerous snakes in the high country, and the only resident that I would have to endure was a harmless carpet python that lived in the attic and kept the bungalow free of mice and rats. I can remember getting revenge on those nurses on my return to Colombo.

The bungalow was in a gorgeous location, across the valley from Adam's Peak, which has a religious background for those of the Buddhist faith. We would see torchlight processions winding up the slopes to the Peak, while hearing the wild elephants trumpeting in the jungles between. By Buddhist tradition, Adam's Peak has a rocky indentation at its Peak, which is said to be the footprint of Buddha when he stepped from the Indian continent.

(FOOTNOTE regarding extra-terrestrial visitors: I find it interesting that there are three places in the world and which I have visited, where 'footsteps" in rock are celebrated by religious sects as being connected with prophets and are believed to be symbols of their departure, perhaps to their heaven. These are Adam's Peak (Buddha); the Temple of the Rock- in Jerusalem (Mohamad's horse); and the ex-Monastery on the Mount of Olives –Jerusalem (Christ). In his book, "Chariots of the Gods" Erich van Daniken suggests that these 'Footsteps' are actually small craters burnt into the rock by the exhaust blasts of inter-planetary rockets which visited Earth from other parts of Space thousands of years earlier.)

The planter, Mervyn, lived alone in a beautiful Company bungalow. He had three house boys to look after him. He

12. Ceylon (Sri Lanka) 1950

would start work at six in the morning by supervising the planting; we would breakfast together at about eight, and then he would spend some time in the tea factory, returning to "morning tiffin" at about eleven. This would be followed by a period of office work, until lunch was served at about one. After lunch he would retire for his kip, going to bed properly, pyjamas and all. He would then rise, and bathe and dress for dinner (black tie, etc.) following this procedure even if he was not going out to dinner or to spend an evening at the Club.

He was but a typical man from a typical British middle class background, but he feared the consequences of lowering his standards in dress or lifestyle. He insisted that I did nothing that would diminish the prestige of this (eccentric) British way of life. "Going Native" was the worst thing a true white colonist could do and was viewed as a hideous treacherous crime — a great contrast to the behaviour of young people visiting such countries these days.

The climate was fantastic. During the day the temperature would be in the mid-twenties, and when it was not in the Monsoon season, every day was sunny and beautiful. At sunset as the evening cooled, the house boys would light a wonderful big open log fire and start up the diesel generator. If we did not go to the Club or go to friends for dinner, Mervyn and I would listen to music by the fireside, play cards, or just read before going to bed.

The Club itself was perhaps typical of hundreds in the

View of Adam's Peak, Maskelia, Sri Lanka.

Commonwealth, and was modelled on similar clubs in England. Where ever the British went, they would create a place that would emulate the life style of the middle class back home, dedicated to socialising and cricket and rugby. In this Club was the remnant of Colonialism, and although the nation had been independent for some years there were actually very few members who were not British. I wonder if things are different now, sixty years later.

Mervyn had something like 30,000 Tamils on the plantation, including children, living in the 'Lines' as he called them. The nearest police station was at Hatton, about 60 plus kilometres away, and thus he really was the only local authority and was trusted by the "natives" to sit in judgement on all sorts of disputes. He would perch himself on a special wicker chair out on the veranda and hold court. His judgements were accepted and based simply on plain common sense and fair play, and without any knowledge of the Law. I am sure things have probably changed since then but this was a typical hangover from the old colonial days, when the white man ruled without question.

After a stay of perhaps three weeks, he took me in his sports car back to Colombo, but even on that trip he insisted in booking us into a Government Rest House for the usual afternoon nap. This was also something of a ritual left over from the old days of Empire and it was not for the last of the British recruits to change it.

I went back to the Hospital in Colombo and there the Doctors decided that I should return to England, and possibly end my career as a seafarer. I did the trip to London, but there the Doctors could not give Saint Line any justification for getting rid of me. I just had to wait for a ship.

Tea Planter's cottage in Ceylon (Sri Lanka)

The time waiting for a suitable passage to London was spent mainly with the Padre of the Seamen's Mission, and I often accompanied him on visits to ships of various nations in the harbour anchorage. Even if he did not know a particular language, he covered this up by sharing smokes and alcohol. This is why I went with him — I could make sure he got home safely.

13. My return to England.

Eventually a passage to U.K. was found for me aboard the P & O passenger vessel "Corfu." She and the "Canton" were smaller than other well-known ships in the P&O passenger fleet, and these two ships shared the run between London and Hong Kong. They were both 'one class' ships,

Other passengers joining the ship were various British families, returning to UK after the recent granting of independence to the ex-Colonies in Hong Kong, Malaysia, and Ceylon. Other passengers included various international

P & O passenger vessel "Corfu."

Missionaries and their families, a few local students bound for British Universities under the wonderful Commonwealth Colombo Plan, and a few world travellers.

{**Posh** : Crossing the Arabian Sea, I was told that the word POSH originated on that leg, meaning Port Out, Starboard Home, the preferred bookings made by influential passengers to make the most of the cooling Trade winds in the days before air conditioning. I have no idea whether this was true.}

On sighting the South Coast of England, I was reminded of Kipling's poem about 'the Giants' as he named the various coastal lighthouses. In the poem a view of these was promised to a dying child, born of British parents in India, and being brought to England to die.

Home again — In London :

Eventually, we berthed at Tilbury and I was greeted as a conquering explorer by my adoring Mother, even though I had only been away for about eight months. It was interesting to me that in that time I had already seen more of the World than my elder brother John, although he had been in the Royal Navy for something like five years.

My insular Mother was of the opinion that anybody who did not live in England, or was not a white citizen of the Commonwealth, was totally uncivilised, (Cannibals started at Calais) so little parcels of razor blades, fruit cake, and

13. My return to England.

even chocolate, kept following me around the World by sea mail and were ravaged by months in the Tropics, if they caught up with me at all.

Naturally, I was still indentured to the Saint Line, and after many medical examinations they could find no reason to get rid of me. Therefore, because none of their ships was due back to UK for a while, it was decided that I should attend King Edward nautical college instead of doing nothing.

I had already some seagoing time, and I was therefore considered too experienced to go with the pre-sea students, so I was included with the older students studying for their Second Mate's certificates. These young men were much older than I was, but I soon settled in with them, and quickly learnt their bad habits!

I remember that among my fellow students were a few New Zealanders who had been Cadets aboard the sailing vessel Pamir, requisitioned by their Government from the Finns during WW2, and sailed in the Southern Oceans for the duration. These lads wanted to obtain a 'square rig endorsement" for their Certificates, but the British had only a meagre supply of sailing ship seafarers who were qualified to examine them and were hard pressed to supply such men for this purpose.

One of these young men, Warwick Dunsford, known as "Dropper", became a firm friend and so remained over the years until he died in Auckland in 2016. His nickname was gained when he dropped a spanner from high on the Pamir's mizzen mast and which only narrowly missed hitting the Chief Officer below.

Because of my fairly unique situation, the College decided that I should concentrate on 'principles' of Nautical Astronomy rather that the 'practical' factors of navigation. It was on this knowledge thus gained that my later business of teaching basic astronomy to Victorian school children was based.

Such an easy existence could not last forever, and all good things have to come to an end. It was therefore arranged that I would work my passage aboard the 'Clan Cumming' as a supernumerary, sailing from Liverpool to Durban in South Africa and there join the 'Saint Bernard'

Voyage to Durban as a Supernumerary.

The voyage as a supernumerary aboard the Clan Liner was not particularly noteworthy, except that she was a modern post-war ship and everything in our quarters seemed luxurious compared to the rather spartan conditions aboard the Saint Gregory, which was built during the height of the War.

While on passage around the Cape of Good Hope, and during the dinner break the evening before arrival in Durban, the ship started to vibrate so badly that the whistle lanyard was jerked and the siren gave intermittent blasts. This is the same signal as that sounded for an emergency,

13. My return to England.

causing a sudden evacuation of the saloon, and something akin to panic among some of the Indian crew.

There was actually no real emergency. The starboard propeller had shed a blade, causing such an in-balance and severe vibration until that engine was stopped. From that time onwards, the ship proceeded to Durban at a reduced speed, where it was to be repaired after final discharge of cargo.

I signed off the Clan Cummings on arrival, and transferred to the 'Saint Bernard', although this was only a short term posting, because the 'Saint Gregory' came into port soon afterwards, and I was then transferred back to her.

Ocean Liner Clan Cummings.

14. Durban — South Africa

Not only was Durban well equipped with facilities for ship repairs and dry-docking, which was the reason that the Saint Bernard was there, but it was one of the main African ports for the export of coal. One of the main shareholders in Saint Line was also the prime owner of coal mines in South Africa, so therefore it was a useful connection for these ships, when shipping was depressed and cargos were otherwise hard to come by. The coal loading berths were located at an area known as The Bluff. Because the area was once riddled with snakes, many mongeese had been imported from India. One of these creatures stowed way when we sailed, as mentioned in a later chapter called "The maritime menagerie"

I spent a total of about six weeks in Durban. After two weeks aboard the Saint Bernard, my old ship the Saint Gregory came in for the same dry docking and to load coal, so I was transferred back to her. After dry docking, we loaded a full cargo of coal for Hong Kong. It was a happy time altogether. I was adopted by the family of one of the harbour Pilots, learnt to surf, although terrified by the huge (to me) waves; watched some cricket between England and South Africa, and played in a couple of cricket matches between seamen from the Mission and local youth clubs. I was a pretty canny spin bowler in those days.

My outstanding memory was of the Padre at the Flying Angel Mission to Seamen. Mr Precious was his name, and a man fully dedicated to his calling. Prior to being ordained, he had been a Chief Officer with Clan Line, so he knew how to handle sailors, and spoke their language, whatever their age or nationality. Because of the happy time, a treasured memory of Christmas 1949 will live on.

In fact, at a family gathering back in England that Christmas, a dear Aunt asked my Mother where I was spending the festive occasion. Her answer – "Charles is having a lovely time in Durban. He is being entertained by the "Fallen" Angels there"

This was in the days before Apartheid became a political football worldwide, and the colour bar was just accepted as a way of life, rather like in the USA at that time. It was a hangover from the Colonial era.

The things I remember most about Durban from my time there, were the rickshaws pulled by half naked Zulus dressed mainly by coloured light globes, the colour bar, and the wonderful Playbox cinema, where the side walls were dressed as an old English village, while stars shone above, and artificial clouds would drift across the roof, being painted on a roll of cellophane. The audience could lie back on wicker stretchers and drink glasses of 'Cape Smoke.' as the local brandy and dry ginger was called. It all seemed very, very civilised, as long as you were white.

My pay was so low as a Cadet, I remember that when we sailed from Durban, I was over eight weeks in debt to the ship.

I have never returned to Durban, but I have fond memories of my weeks there. (On a business trip later in the 70's to South Africa, I visited Capetown, Johanesburg, and Paarl, but nothing diminished my memories of Durban, which I visited as a young apprentice seafarer so many years ago.)

Fools and Firemen — Cadets relaxing .

15. Durban to Hong Kong

"Fire down Below."

After this pleasant break in port I left Durban in debt to the ship for about two month's pay.

We had loaded a full cargo of coal for Hong Kong. This did not take long and was achieved by big railway trucks loaded with coal being lifted and then physically turned over for their coal to be poured into hoppers and thence into the ship.

Because it was to be a long trip, and the cost of coal in Durban was relatively low, we loaded extra bunkers on deck. This was spread each side of the Bunker Hatches and found its way under the Boat Deck, and for a time it somewhat restricted our passage along the alleyways on each side of the ship. Jumping over this coal in my haste to get to the saloon for dinner one evening, it caused me to crack my head on the deck head beams, requiring stiches and leaving a scar that I carry to this day. It also led to an abbreviated romance with a rather delightful hospital nurse.

It was an uneventful trip across the Indian Ocean and we stopped briefly at Singapore to change part of the Chinese crew. Proceeding later through the Malacca strait, the narrow channel between Malaysia and Indonesia, a hawk dropped a snake onto the bridge, giving rise to the story within the 'maritime menagerie' collection below.

We were half way between Singapore and Hong Kong when it was discovered that the coal in Number 2 Hold was on fire, apparently ignited by spontaneous combustion. There was not a lot we could do, and to open up the hold would only allow oxygen to fuel the fire. Instead we removed some of the hold ventilators and covered up those remaining, to bar the entry of oxygen. The ship's only fire-fighting equipment fitted was that all holds could be flooded with steam. This was utilised, and the subsequent water being extracted via the bilges, even though some of the bilge pumps were blocked by the accumulated coal dust.

The fire was fortunately thus contained until our arrival in Hong Kong about a week later, where the trained fire-fighters could handle the situation, while at the same time discharge of the smouldering coal took place.

Spontaneous combustion of coal (and some other types of cargo including types of wool) has a historical maritime background, causing the loss of many fine ships over the years, and has now led to the imposition of various International Laws regarding the carriage of hazardous cargo.

Note. This concern has recently come to light by the number of ships fully loaded with coal but forced to anchor off Chinese ports while awaiting the resolution of a political argument between China and Australia.

16. Nauru. (Gilbert & Ellice Islands)

The Phosphate Island

After discharging the coal and surveying any resultant damage from the fire, the crew and apprentices spent happy hours cleaning the Holds, while the ship proceeded under ballast to Nauru, in the then named Gilbert & Ellice Islands, to load phosphate fertiliser for Australia.

Nauru, in common with its neighbour, Ocean Island, is a very small coral island. Both are situated near the Equator, and the high quality phosphate fertiliser mined there is simply bird droppings that have accumulated over centuries. The story of how the phosphate was discovered and of

Phosphate Island of Nauru.

the history of the British Phosphate Commission is told in a history book published by the BPC. In simple terms it all started by a closer examination of a piece of rock used as a door-stopper in an island residence.

One point worth noting is that the formation of the living coral making up the reef is virtually vertical, and the depth of the sea surrounding the island varies from a few feet in the lagoons, to an almost sheer drop to over a thousand meters. During World War Two, Japanese forces occupied both islands, but failed to export a single load of the valuable phosphate, because the British had destroyed the mooring buoys, and the Japanese failed to understand the mooring systems used to combat the strong equatorial currents in such an extreme depth of water. The secret used by the British before and after the War was simply based on the buoyancy of the huge buoys, held with a single deep anchor, and then using breast moorings to keep the system in place.

It is a pretty frail system for all that, and if the ocean currents were too strong or if the weather was adverse, ships were forced to lie off and "drift". The BPC ships did have priority over chartered vessels, because they carried water and stores for the island, but the rules still applied. Later in life, when I was working on the Tri-Ellis, the longest drift we then endured was 41 days, and we were forced to sail for Honiara in the Solomon Islands to replenish the supply of water.

The face of the reef is full of small caves that contain,

16. Nauru. (Gilbert & Ellice Islands)

among other maritime creatures, a multitude of octopus, viewed as a delicacy by the local people. To catch these, divers worked in pairs and without equipment. The first man dives, thrusts his arm into a likely cave, and allows the creature inside to fasten itself to his arm. The second diver thence goes down and proceeds to pull both the captured diver and the creature free, and all three then return to the surface,

Two special conveyors delivered the phosphate quickly, and in about twelve hours a total of around ten thousand tons of crushed rock was loaded. During this time, the ship was totally enveloped in a cloud of white dust, to be washed away when the ship sailed later that night. We were told that this dust had no effect upon health. After over sixty years, I am still awaiting the proof.

{Later, when serving aboard the Tri-Ellis we used to amaze the passengers after we had spent some time on deck in this cloud of dust, by clutching a handful of phosphate and then holding the loaded hand to the mouth, and then coughing, caused a cloud of dust to fly as though from our lungs }

17. Nauru to Australian Ports

Newcastle, Port Kembla, Geelong, Adelaide. Port Lincoln.

At the time I am writing about, during the 1950's, the Australian coast was crowded with shipping. Ships for both cargo and coastal passenger trade were regularly employed. Road transport was in its infancy. Rail transport was dis-jointed, mainly because of the variations of rail gauges throughout the Commonwealth. They were a living and historical example of State Government parochialism.

Transport was needed to carry all types of goods between Cities, and also the raw materials like coal and ore from mining centres to industrial converters. Australian owned ships could not meet the demand, and consequently many foreign ships, mainly British tramp ships, were under charter in what was called the "Slave Trade".

The British tramps seemed to be predominately owned by Andrew Weir (Bank Line) or the Ropner Group (named 'Pool or 'By.) and these were manned mainly by the dregs of British maritime crews. Many of these sailors ended up by being deported, if they had not previously deserted (jumped) their ships beforehand.

Australian sailors, strongly unionised and politically influential, had working conditions that were the envy of the world. They even seemed to have an unofficial uniform — dark blue shirt, light coloured jeans, and always a white floppy cap. A wide belt with a sheath knife was a requisite, and they were the only citizens allowed by Law to wear these knives in public as a 'tool of trade.'

Our cargo from Nauru was evenly distributed between Newcastle and Port Kembla, which then was only a small seaport in NSW, Geelong in Victoria, and Port Adelaide in South Australia.

Newcastle in NSW has been a main coal port ever since the early days of Australian trade, with coal mines situated in the Hunter Valley and even in the days of sailing ships coal exports to places all over the world was an important component of Australia's exports. We took on coal bunkers while there, loading the coal bunkers with slow water driven cranes that took nearly as long as discharging the part cargo of phosphate. These were days where "time" did not seem so important.

I can remember a Saturday afternoon when we were lashed outboard of a "Slave Trader" a Ropner tramp called "Herronspool". The Liverpool- Irish crew had spent some hours drinking and this drunken mob had terrified our Chinese crew. They were also seen chasing their own officers around the decks while being armed with fire axes. Their sport was interrupted by car loads of tough Australian policemen and many of these sailors were locked up until sober.

The last of the phosphate was discharged in Adelaide and we then were fitted out to load grain in Port Lincoln for Madras in India with the complicated "Shifting Boards" so necessary if a ship is to be loaded with grain.

Grain has a very low "angle of rest" and is virtually like water. It can shift easily when a ship rolls even to small angle and many ships were known to have capsized because their cargo had shifted. There is an additional problem with grain, because it can 'settle down', and move below the height of any fore-and-aft constructed bulkhead. Therefore the holds have to be fitted with constructed timber "feeder bins" which would keep the hold topped up during a voyage.

Fitting this array of timber shifting boards could take an army of carpenters several days to prepare, and in addition, the bilges had to have burlap tacked over them, so that the grain could not clog the pumps in any emergency. All this preparation was done in Adelaide before we sailed for Port Lincoln.

As a result, we were some time in Port Adelaide, and I have some special memories of happy times there, especially the Saturday night dances at the Port Adelaide Town hall and overcoming the strict local 6 o'clock drinking laws by signing as 'bone fide travellers.

SEQUEL. Many years later, when we were looking for the ideas for the development of the Melbourne Maritime Museum, I visited the South Australian Maritime Museum, one of the finest in Australia. To develop this museum the State had taken over most of the previous Port Adelaide maritime area and achieved a spectacular historical display. This result was largely due to the creative skills and illusions created by a movie designer rather than a traditional museum designer.

Note: It was during this time in Adelaide that the experience with rats happened. These events are detailed in the story entitled 'Maritime Menagerie' below.

18. The Maritime Menagerie.

I suppose that every sailor has memories of the various non-human creatures that were his shipmates, and with which they had spent some time, either pleasurable or otherwise. The stories told below tell of my own such experiences.

1. The Copra Bugs

I thought I would write this chapter after discussion at the Yacht Club bar during the weekly "light swinging" session held at lunchtime each Saturday. Another ex-seafarer asked me casually if I had ever made the acquaintance of those dear little shiny fiends — the Copra Beetles. We therefore realized that we shared this memory. My friend had loaded copra (and the bugs) in Indonesia for Liverpool, where the Lever Company extracted the coconut oil to make Palmolive soap and similar products.

My own experience was on the other side of the world. In the 1950's during the Korean War we were under charter to an American company, States Marine Inc. and loaded army supplies in Californian ports for the conflict. The return voyage was financed by loading copra, actually dried coconut husks, in the Philippines for discharge in California.

It was a pleasant task loading the copra, anchoring off small islands, with the cargo coming out in barges, and the sacks of copra lifted aboard in nets, to be slit and bled into the holds. It took many days and many islands to fill the ship, with little cargo supervision needed and that gave us a chance to explore and have the adventures ashore that young sailors like to have, usually aided by Manila Rum and San Miguel beer.

The down side to this was that for every ton of copra loaded, we loaded about a million Copra Beetles. These are armour plated, shiny little beasts, usually about 3mm long, and armed with a sharp spear of a tail, which they delighted in using on bare skin at every opportunity.

The ship was covered. The white superstructure was blackened by the silent throng of bugs. That was bad enough, but they were everywhere. — in our clothes, in our beds, and even sharing our cereals at breakfast with the more usual weevils. There seemed to be no poison in their stings, but living with those vicious beasts was like having hundreds of inoculations each day.

From memory, the voyage from the Philippines to San Francisco took around 20 days, and these little darlings did their utmost to make these voyages memorable.

The most amazing part of the experience though was that as the last of the copra was sucked ashore, so were the last of the beetles. That solved our problem — until we went back for more.

2. Seabirds

Everybody associates the sea and its shore with mewing seagulls, cantankerous gannets, and birds diving for fish, etc. At sea, it was a daily event to see the birds swooping on the galley scraps when they were thrown overboard.

One of the greatest timewasting pleasures in the Southern Hemisphere is to watch those wonderful albatrosses, some with wing spans of over three meters, effortlessly gliding over the waves and rarely moving their wings. They are truly the souls of departed seafarers, as figured in mythology.

I came to know them at close quarters when working on a New Zealand based oceanographic ship, where we would capture them and add ring tags, so that they could be tracked for science. Scientists use more electronic methods these days.

One memory stands out when the "Saint Gregory" was on the run between California and Korea. Somewhere in the Pacific we ran into a cyclone, with the usual combination of strong winds and huge seas plus the feeling of going nowhere with the ship hove to and weathering the storm.

It must have been the migratory season for flocks of little grey-blue birds, of species unknown to me.

Here in this vast and seemingly boundless ocean they sighted our ship, and saw a haven and refuge from the storm. Literally thousands of these birds came to rest their weary wings aboard. These creatures migrate incredible distances, half way across the world, but in this case they were exhausted in fighting the storm, and many just fell asleep where they landed.

It so happened that when we were last in San Francisco we cadets had updated all the tins of sweetened condensed milk emergency rations stored in the four lifeboats and we kept the old tins for personal use. This meant we were well equipped with the old milk, and these little birds reaped the rewards.

I had two ports in my cabin, both facing aft, so even though the weather was stormy, I was able to have them open. My home became home to a few of these birds. They would rest on my bookshelf or my fan guard and became really quite tame when they were not asleep. It was a bit like a story from the Disney film about Uncle Remus…"**There's a bluebird on my shoulder**"……Do you remember that song?

The storm lasted for about three days, and then gradually moderated. As the wind dropped, so the birds departed to continue their long lonely flight — to where…..?

3. The Ship's Pets

On board the "Saint Gregory" we had both an anonymous cat and a dog named Susie. The problem with such shipboard pets is that they pose a constant problem with quarantine officials wherever we went. If you arrived with an animal, you had to have an animal when you sailed.

Susie the dog was really no problem. She was a home loving animal and everyone made a fuss of her. She had long ago adopted the Half Deck, the cadets' quarters, as her home.

She was clean and house trained, with a tray of sand for her business. No problems existed.

The cat was different. Cats are independent and wanderers. Like true sailors, they had the urge to explore ashore and it was virtually impossible to keep them aboard. Therefore a few occasions arose where on sailing day no cat could be found. The solution — tell the cadets to get a cat, any cat, just to show the quarantine people.

Efforts were made to secure the same type and colour, but that was not always achieved. We just had to hope that it was not realized by the Port Officials that our cat was a ginger Tom on arrival and had gone through a sexual realignment and colour change over the period of our visit.

Then there was a mongoose. It came aboard in Durban where the locals had imported them from India to combat the snakes on the water front. This particular one was a stowaway, and only discovered after we had sailed. It became very tame — starvation coaxed it into friendliness — but it remained somewhat aloof from true adoption. On arrival in a port we had to hope it was not noticed or if it was, that it would still be aboard when we sailed.

I can't remember where, but eventually it "jumped ship" somewhere, but as its existence had not been noted, there were no repercussions.

However, even the dog, Susie, had her moments ! She had adopted the cadets and was a superb guard for the Half Deck. She became my shadow, and was even allowed to keep bridge watches with me.

Elsewhere in my memoirs I have recounted the occasion that two of us swam the Suez Canal so we could boast we had swum from Asia to Africa. What I had also related, was that half way back to the ship we met Susie swimming to meet us. Her motherly instincts had told her we needed to be looked after.

4. The Migrant Dog.

By now you will realize that dogs and I get on well together — kindred spirits perhaps. It was when I was Third mate aboard the "Papanui" on a voyage from UK to New Zealand, that this episode took place. The first port of call in New Zealand was Wellington.

We often carried livestock, but on this occasion we had a dog. We were told that the family and their children had

18. The Maritime Menagerie.

migrated to New Zealand and had left the dog with friends in Yorkshire. The dog missed his young master, and was pining away, in a bad temper and with no appetite.

Eventually the people of the village, had raised enough money to send the dog out to rejoin the family, and our ship was chosen to do the job. A special kennel was provided on the Boat Deck and the Second Cook was told off to look after the dog. A bad choice, and the first time the cook took him food, the dog bit the hand that fed him. Labour was immediately withdrawn, and dog loving Charley (me) gained the job.

The voyage lasted around the usual 35 days via Panama, and the dog and I became great mates. He lived mainly in my cabin, and was allowed on the bridge when I was on watch. He did have a bad feeling about the captain and only allowed him on the bridge with great suspicion. Bad temper was displayed to most of the crew, and I was left usually in peace.

Eventually we arrived at Wellington. The local media had been briefed about the dog's background, and were warned that this dog was bad tempered and was almost a man eater.

We berthed and the family with members of the Press clambered aboard. They were assembled at the after end of the boat deck, and when all was ready I was to arrive with the dog at the other end of the deck.

The dog was nervous and barking, and then.... He noticed his young master standing there with the family. The tail wagged and I let him go. He rushed into familiar arms, and then went around licking everybody's hand. Love was the only thing he knew from then on.

5. Livestock

It was quite common in the Fifties for good breeding animals to be purchased by farmers in Australia, and then shipped out from the UK by sea, aboard on ships like the "Saint Gregory".

On this particular voyage from UK to Australia we carried sixteen of these fine beasts, a mixture of ginger Short Horns and black and white Herefords — the latter are animals with the biggest span of intimidating horns I have ever seen.

Wooden stalls were constructed on the open after deck, eight on each side of the number four and five hatches. A cattleman was appointed for the voyage, to be assisted by .....you guessed it.....the cadets, who always got the jobs nobody else wanted. The cattleman discovered the delights of Duty Free whiskey soon after sailing, and we were forced to become substituted experts at watering, feeding, and mucking out.

Quite a good relationship built up between the animals and the Cadets, though not without some trepidation on my part. I remember one huge Shorthorn bull would play the pressure game with me. Whenever I lowered a bucket

18. The Maritime Menagerie.

Cattle stalls stove in by Monsoon.

of water into his stall, he would lean forward, pinning my arm to the timber railing. I can still remember those big liquid eyes scoffing at my attempts to break free. I wished him well and like to think that perhaps I got my revenge later via a Big Mac.

All went well until after we bunkered at Aden and sailed into the Indian Ocean. It was July and during the months of June to September the heat of the Northern Summer creates a seasonal low pressure system over Asia, causing the South West Monsoon to blow across the Indian Ocean. This is a steady 30 knot wind with quite a high running sea.

Passing from the lee of Socotra, off the Horn of Africa, was like turning on a tap. The ship started rolling, and shipping heavy seas, quickly causing the fragile cattle stalls on the starboard side to be broken up by the waves crashing aboard. Naturally, the poor animals on that side of the ship were terrified, so "all hands on deck" was the call to rescue them and shift them to the Port side in the lee. This I should add was after night fall, and was a monumental task that few of us would ever forget. We were sailors, not cowboys!

Perhaps you can picture the scene. The ship pitching and rolling heavily, green seas crashing aboard, loose timber from the broken stalls flying around, sometimes with a terrified animal still attached, and all illuminated by the mast flood lights shining through the sea spray.

It was during this adventure that I was to become known as "El Toriodor". I was tugging on the halter of this huge Hereford cow, and the Chief Officer and Sparks (The Radio Officer) each had a shoulder on her buttocks. The ship lurched to Port, and with a rush I found those huge horns bearing down on me. I managed to side step with the aplomb of a trained bull fighter as this massive animal came thundering by, though badly bruising my foot with her hoof on the way.

By dawn, all the animals were doubled up in the lee stalls, with no severe injuries to man and beast. The cook prepared extra eggs and bacon for breakfast as a just reward.

A night to remember, perhaps, but it was all in the day's work for a young officer cadet.

6. Rats

Rodents have a long history aboard ships. In the Middle Ages the fleas on rats caused the spread of plague, the Black

Death, across Europe. Since that time, Authorities have tried to make sure that the rat contingent of any ship are kept aboard by Rat Guards, conical metal discs, fixed on every mooring line, or else by sacking covered with Stockholm Tar and lashed around each mooring line.

It was mandatory that every ship should be fumigated regularly, each compartment sealed up and filled, in my days anyway, with cyanide gas. The crew then had to wait for a safety all-clear from the chemist and his helpers who had committed the casualties to the rodent happy hunting ground.

I remember when serving on the "Durham", we had undertaken this procedure in Falmouth, and afterwards loaded in various UK ports for Australia. This took about four weeks, and eventually we sailed. It was not really until we reached the warmer weather of the Mediterranean that we started looking at each other suspiciously, wondering where the smell in the Officers' Lounge was originating.

By the time we were in mid Red Sea, the stink was unbearable, and a full scale investigation carried out. When the armchairs and settees were searched we found a multitude of dead and rotting rats up among the springs. These last casualties were soon dealt with, and the evening chess and cribbage clubs could resume without mutual suspicion.

7. Rats and Pants!

I actually had a closer encounter with rats during my

apprenticeship, aboard the "Saint Gregory". We cadets shared the Half Deck, a deck house on the boat deck. These quarters consisted of three cabins, a mess room, a bathroom, and a small pantry, and were originally built as quarters for the army gunners placed aboard each merchant ship during World War Two.

We were in Adelaide discharging cargo. I was off duty one Saturday afternoon, and went shopping for some much needed new underwear. (That need is another story!) I returned to the ship, opened my parcels, and left the contents on my bunk, but when I returned, I found that two pairs of new underpants were missing. My accusations to the other cadets brought pleas of innocence, so this all remained a mystery.

It was my usual habit to read in bed before going to sleep, and if it was available, I would eat a little fruit — just to keep the scurvy at bay. Above my head was a narrow shelf, and that particular night I had left an apple core and orange peel there so as to avoid getting out of bed. I switched off the light and snuggled down to sleep.

It was some time later that I awoke to feel something on my head, and illuminated by the light of mast lights shining through my porthole, I realized there was a rat attacking the remains of the fruit and using my head as a sort of staging. I will never know which of us moved the fastest.

Later as we all awoke there was a shout from one of the other Cadets — " Hey — come and look at this " We crowded

18. The Maritime Menagerie.

into our small toilet, and there, swimming valiantly and trying to get a grip on the smooth china sides of the bowel, was a big, brown rat. "Flush the toilet" somebody said, but alas, our friend was too big or too buoyant, and repeated flushing attempts failed.

This was a crisis of classic proportions. Nobody was going to risk their tender parts with those teeth by using the bowl. Something had to be done.

It was a courageous member of our group, who, after much preparation — wearing heavy work gloves, high neck pull-over, balaclava, and rope yarn lashings around his sleeves, and sea boots — thrust his hand into the bowel, grabbed the rat, rushed to the doorway, and threw the rodent into the harbour. We watched it swimming around until the hash hammer went for lunch-time. The power of survival is strong. Having spent all night trapped in a toilet bowl and now swimming in Adelaide Harbour, it just would not drown. That rat probably lived to tell its offspring of the dangers of modern sanitation.

That was not the end of the story. We decided that should search our whole quarters, but only once dressed in the manner I described above — we all know that rats can climb trouser legs with disastrous effects upon matrimonial prospects. Anyway, to cut a long story short, the hunt concluded when we lifted the grating under the pantry sink, to find a rats' nest — five little baby rats nestling together. What was the nest made of? You guessed it — my new and missing knickers !

Why did I need new under pants — now it can be told.

Every Sunday, the Captain of the ship would conduct his Rounds, and inspection of every part of the ship for reasons of safety and hygiene. The Captain of this ship had an obsession about the cleanliness of the Cadets — he would want to see what washing needed doing and if it had been done properly. Washing clothes was not my forte so I would go to extreme lengths to hide these things from him — under the mattress, behind the chest of drawers, all sorts of places, but wherever I hid them — he would find them and I would suffer.

One of the regular jobs for the Cadets was to polish the ship's brass — the bells, the binnacles, and the ship's steam whistle. With my youthful ingenuity I worked out that if I put my dirty washing in the brass cleaning drawer the Captain would not find them.

This ruse worked OK for one Sunday but to my horror I later found that my best underwear had been used to clean the ship's steam whistle. I hadn't warned my shipmates, and paid the price, to the later benefit of the rat family.

Footnote,

What happened to the baby rats? Well — our Chinese sailors had some strange ideas about dietary delicacies.

19. The Crickets at Portarlington

It was Christmas time in 1975, and I had recently launched my yacht "Isa Lei". We enjoyed a traditional Christmas Day at home and then on Boxing Day we moved the whole family to Mornington, where the boat was kept on moorings during the summer season. I was a keen member of the Yacht Club there, and have fond memories of those years of my membership, for both racing and cruising.

We had decided to spend a few days living on the boat, cruising the Bay and generally relaxing. We took the two children; Jane would have been about six years old and John was about two.

We sailed the next day down to Portsea and chanced to meet up with the Moscow Circus. We were staying at the Portsea Hotel and met the Russian "Foot Jugglers" at lunch by Jane showing off her large Teddy Bear. We later took six of them out for an afternoon's fishing and were given a free pass to the Circus, which we used later when we got home. I remember that just after we got them aboard, we were urged to shove off from the pier so as to avoid another person from boarding. It turned out that this was the KVD commissar who's company the other passengers wanted to avoid.

I heard later that the fish they caught were actually cooked in the water jug at their hotel in Melbourne. The next guests in the room must have wondered why their coffee tasted so weird.

We set sail the next day and arrived in the early evening at Portarlington, on our way to Geelong. We found the harbor at Portarlington very crowded with fishing boats and holiday people, but as we were self-contained and the weather was calm, I decided to anchor for the night just near the pier.

It must have been around 1030pm. The children and my wife were fast asleep down below, but I decided to enjoy the warm and placid evening in the cockpit, with a flagon of good wine as company.

Suddenly, I felt a blow on my back, and then another, and then another. Reaching for a torch, I found the cockpit a shining black mass of crawling crickets. But then I found it was not only the cockpit but the whole yacht that was covered and had become a seething world of black, sinister crickets.

I shone the torch down below, and was shocked to find the whole family had been similarly invaded and their beds were covered with the creatures

What should I do? I knew it was only a matter of time before somebody below woke up, and I knew there would be

19. The Crickets at Portarlington

some consequential hysterics when they found themselves covered in crickets.

I first gently woke my wife, and calmed her disbelief by explaining that I would cruise seawards in the hope that these unwanted passengers would leave us for their shore side preference, and all she would have to do is to calm the children if they awoke.

I heaved up the anchor, started the engine, and headed out to sea. I realized soon after I had made a huge miscalculation and that the rest of the cricket swarm saw the boat as a haven in the night, and came aboard the yacht to join their mates and to enjoy the nighttime cruise. They had been blown across the Bay, but instead of making landfall at Portarlington they chose to land on my yacht.

There was nothing for it, but to keep on sailing through the night, with the wind set fair for a return to Mornington. That was a trip I don't think any of us would ever forget. Fortunately the weather remained calm, so that was not a problem, but the crickets were a real one. Every movement would cause a shower of displaced insects, and every time a step was taken, it would generate a squelch of crushed crickets.

We arrived at Mornington at about 8am. I tied up at the small pier and sent my wife and children ashore immediately to ring our friends the Andersons to explain our misfortune. They arrived soon after and Judy Anderson took the family up to their home, while her husband Bill joined me in surveying the boat.

What a scene! I just could not believe it.

The whole boat was a mass of crickets. Every sheet, every coil of rope, all the furled sails, were all full of the black devils. Inspection down below revealed a similar picture. Every locker, all the bedclothes, all the bookshelves, even the closed sail bags showed complete occupancy by crickets. Even the bilges and the engine space were full of these unwelcome lodgers.

Another friend was detailed off to obtain two dozen cans of fly killer, and once we were armed with these, everything aboard was sprayed, the dead crickets disposed of, and all the gear was then piled on to the pier, to be sprayed again. The water around the yacht was black with dead or dying crickets — we must have killed thousands of them.

Once empty, the interior of the boat was given a great spray of the killer stuff, and the dead crickets were shoveled over the side. When we were convinced that we had disposed of all these insects, we started loading the boat again. That took nearly all the rest of the day, and by the time I had put the boat back on its mooring again, there was only time to buy my helpers a beer at the pub before we had dinner at the Andersons.

I realized then how exhausted I was — I had been awake for over thirty-six hours, thanks to all those little black devils.

The Sequel

A couple of years later, and because I wanted to add some gear at the mast head, we lifted the hollow mast by using the Club crane. When the mast came clear of the deck, a neat pile of dead crickets poured out of its interior.

For all that intervening time, the mast had been a memorial to our terrible experience during that night at Portarlington, and an unseen cemetery of long-dead crickets.

My 'Pride and Joy' — Yacht Tempe.

20. Port Lincoln. (And the ship " Mill Hill")

Loading grain for Calcutta — India.

Famous in the earlier years as a regular sailing ship port for loading grain, Port Lincoln is located in the Spencer Gulf of South Australia. In fact Basil Lubbuck's book "The Last of the Grain Racers" gives an interesting description of the port, and the sailing ships that would load there. The Grain Trade was one of the last trades that the sailing ships could compete with steam, even until just after WW2.

At the time we visited there, sailing the short distance from Adelaide, the place was a typical small Australian way-port. A scenic bay, surrounded by the green rolling hills of the Boston Penninsula, and a single wooden jetty, serviced by rail trucks that would bring the grain in bags to the ship's side. Because there was a constant surge from the open sea, the ship was secured by heavy coir rope springs that would absorb the movement. When we were there we saw even a couple of the small schooners that were still trading around the coasts. Those days have now well and truly gone.

Grain these days is transported to the ships in bulk and loaded by elevators. Ten thousand tons can be loaded in a few hours, and specially constructed ships can carry three times that load. However, we loaded grain a few times in the old way, always very slow and laborious, with the grain delivered in bags. The ships derricks would lift a sling of ten bags, and deposit them on to a prepared platform of similar bags on the hold hatches. The bags would then be slit open, allowing the grain to fall into the hold below through gaps left in the spaced hatch boards. Any arrival of rain would interrupt the loading, and the holds had to be covered. I am not sure if this was to keep the cargo dry or for the benefit of the wharf labourers.

It was during our stay in Port Lincoln that the British ship "Mill Hill" was towed into port, with a list to starboard of over 60 degrees. So acute was the list that although she was only partially loaded, such was her freeboard that her starboard bulwark was under water. The "Mill Hill" was a wartime American " Liberty" ship now under the British flag, and owned by Counties Shipping, a Greek owned group that had bought up many of these surplus ships after the war was over.

Apparently she had loaded a part-cargo of zinc concentrates in Whyalla (another Gulf port) and was intending to load further in Adelaide. Because of the short voyage across the Gulf the cargo had not been secured. During the voyage, a sudden storm caused the cargo to shift and Number two hatch to be stove in. While trying to fix the damage, the Chief Officer and two sailors were swept to their death.

The ship was anchored off shore but the local stevedores would not handle the cargo to correct the list until negotiations about "danger money" were finalised. So meantime this damaged ship was a local tourist attraction. For a short while we apprentices earnt good money by taking tourists out for a close view of that ship in our motorised lifeboat, until finally the local Harbour Master pointed out that we were not licenced to carry paying passengers and we were forced to desist.

This action was obviously prompted by local interests who we had upset, but it was very lucrative for us apprentices while it lasted. We all needed that welcomed extra money.

We enjoyed terrific hospitality from the local inhabitants, in common with that enjoyed in all the smaller ports of Australia and New Zealand. The world was smaller

Shipwreck of ship ' Mill Hill'

in those days, and people in these small communities welcomed contact with the outside world — personalized by visiting ships.

One occasion I do remember was being taken to a farm outside Port Lincoln for a BBQ. I was told off to collect wood for the fire and when lifting a large log, I disturbed a sleeping blue-tongued lizard. I was told afterwards that these were harmless and that many children adopted them as pets, although at the time I thought it was a crocodile, and ran for my life.

I have such pleasant memories of Port Lincoln, and it was with some regret that we completed loading, and sailed for Calcutta in India.

21. Calcutta — Refit and Coal for Melbourne

The voyage from South Australia was pretty uneventful, with typical weather in the Bight, big Southern Ocean swells but only moderate winds, and then across the Indian Ocean, until we were virtually within the delta of Calcutta's river — the River Hoogli.

We had picked up the Pilot just before a cyclonic storm broke, forcing us to anchor in the delta at late evening because of the blinding rain and general poor visibility. I remember the dreadful, dark, murky overcast scene and the high, unbearable humidity together with the howling wind. The Pilot himself was British, obviously an old-time Colonial, and he had with him a native 'bearer" or servant, employed just to carry his small brief case and to cater for his every need.

We had a Pilot's Cabin, on the lower bridge deck, but the poor, barely dressed, bearer, had to sleep outside the Pilot's door on a wet, wind swept deck, just in case the Pilot would want something during the night.

At daylight the next morning, when the weather had

moderated, we had to hang off an anchor with wires, break open the cable, and then flake ten fathoms of cable ready to be taken aft, to use as a stern mooring. The River Hoogli has a famous fierce tidal bore, and to prevent ships from breaking free, anchor cables are used for mooring. Regular traders, like the Brocklebank or British India liners, have anchor cables fitted aft as a permanent feature.

After we berthed, hordes of labourers descended on the ship to unload the grain and dismantle the shifting boards. With so many strangers wandering aboard the ship, we had to make sure that our cabins were locked, and that many parts of the ship were securely guarded.

When all the grain had been discharged the ship was moved into dry-dock for insurance survey and painting. Again the ship was covered with Indian labourers, each armed with a chipping hammer and a scraper, and each had perhaps a designated square meter to work on. Within a few hours the ship was bare metal, then a few hours later just a mass of red lead paint, and finally, a brand new, freshly painted and shining ship would appear.

While all this was going on, The Engineers, working in 40+ degree heat, were executing a necessary boiler survey. It was hot enough on deck, but how those men survived below really beats me.

One memory I have of Calcutta is the multitude of insect life that descended on the ship, attracted by the dock floodlights. Particularly noteworthy were what we called the

21. Calcutta — Refit and Coal for Melbourne

Bombay Charleys, huge and fat cockroaches that were so big that one could almost hear them clunking along the deck.

After five days, our ship sparkling with new paintwork was moved again to a loading berth, to load coal for Melbourne. Again because labour was inexpensive, the loading was done by hand. Planks of wood, for both on and off pedestrian passage, were placed at each hatch, and a constant stream of humanity, of all ages and sexes, each with a basket of coal on their head, would stagger up on deck, drop their load into the hold, and then go to the wharf to get another load and repeat the process.

It sounds so slow, but the work was achieved with minimum breaks for food and rest for the labour, and so within four days we were loaded with ten thousand tons of coal, and ready to sail for Melbourne, Australia.

We were not aware of this at the time, but Australia was then in the grips of nationwide industrial strife, and the coal we carried was to keep the generators in Melbourne working, so that they could continue to keep domestic and industrial power being supplied. We were therefore called "strike breakers" by some Australian unionists.

Me painting draught marks.

22. Melbourne in the Early Fifties

It was almost prophetic that my first visit to Melbourne in 1950 would ultimately see this city as the place that will be my final home and the theatre in which most of my later life would be performed.

This destiny was far removed from our reasons for this first visit. We were in fact unwittingly strike breakers, or more brutally named by the Australian unionists as "Pommy scabs". Obviously, we knew nothing of the political background to our visit, or our reason for bringing coal to Melbourne. It was purely that our ship had been chartered in arrangements made on the other side of the world, and we were simply doing our job.

After the end of WW2, Australia, in common with a lot of the world, was in the grips of political upheaval. Trade Union influence has always been dominant in the country's political scene, but at this stage was being taken over by the extreme Left of the Communist Party. All of business, and particularly the strategic coal mines, were disrupted by strikes and lock-outs. This meant that power generation and gas supplies, together with the whole social fabric of the country, were threatened. The military had been mobilised to mine and distribute coal, while imports, like our shipload of Indian coal from Calcutta, had been purchased to ensure gas and electricity supply.

Melbourne has changed in many ways since 1950 and this was of course well before natural gas was adopted in 1970. Melbourne's gas supplies in those days was manufactured from coal at various gas works throughout the City, with their big gasometers dominating the skyline, as they did in nearly every community throughout the world. Most of Victorian gas works were made redundant and their sites sold in 1970, with the subsequent loss of over 1000 jobs. This happened all over the World, and one of the most famous remaining is the gasometer overlooking the Oval cricket ground in London.

To discharge our cargo, we berthed at the dedicated coaling berth in Victoria Dock, using huge 'grabs' attached to cranes, that released their loads into hoppers feeding rail trucks. In this way, we unloaded ten thousand tons of coal in something like two weeks.

(Side Issue) In writing this I am reminded that wherever there was a gasworks, there would be an attendant sour smell of gas. One of my Father's brothers, known in the Family as our 'Rude Uncle' would always say, when driving past the Croydon Gasworks, "Now's your chance, Fellows !"

It was during this time that I first enjoyed the **Flying Angel Mission to Seamen**, still located to this day in Flinders

Street, and made friends with the then Assistant Padre, Bill Dowd. In those days the Port was crowded with British ships, and the Mission consequently was frequented by poorly paid British cadets — each ship carried two or four cadets, and these were supplemented by the occasional cadet ship with perhaps forty young men training to become ship's officers.

The Seaman's Mission offered a real low cost home-from-home for us penniless youngsters and was a place we could spend off-duty hours playing billiards or table tennis. On Sundays it would arrange trips to the Dandenong Ranges for Devonshire teas of scones with jam and cream, followed by the Sunday night dance with local young ladies. The price for all this was a twenty minute Service in the Mission chapel, a stipend willingly paid towards a debt gratefully sustained.

The last time that I saw Bill Dowd was when I was Third Mate of the passenger ship Rangitata and Bill was bumped into on the dockside at Albert Dock in London, when he was Padre at the Flying Angel mission located there.

The Rona Coal Hulk (now the restored sailing barque Polly Woodside)

I have mentioned previously that our ship Saint Gregory was a coal burning steam ship, so while we were discharging our coal cargo on to the wharf on the starboard side, we also were loading coal bunker fuel from the Rona coal hulk lashed alongside on the port side.

The 'Rona' was one of several ex- sailing ship barges, known as hulks, used for coal fuel bunkering visiting ships. It was a twist of fate that 30 years later I would become the CEO in charge of restoring this old wreck back to her former glory as the Polly Woodside, and the ship would become an iconic reminder to younger generations of the sailing ships and sailors who had helped to create our modern Australia. The Polly Woodside became a good example of the small group of heritage vessels supported in various seaports around the World, and had became the fifth restored ship to be awarded the prized World Heritage Medal.

At that time, 'Rona' was one of many famous sailing ships employed to coal bunker visiting ships, all of which were ultimately to lie rotting in the 'Graveyard' a riverside area located where the Westgate Bridge is today. As visiting ships

The 'Polly Woodside' Before Restoration
— The Coal Hulk 'Rona'

converted to oil fuel, these relics were finally broken up or sunk just outside the Heads in Bass Strait and this could well have been the ultimate fate of Rona but for the intervention of the National Trust and their bold decision to restore her for posterity. Their decision resulted from the enthusiasm of an American mariner who had been instrumental in saving the British sailing ship "Balclutha" which today is a main attraction at the famous Fisherman's Wharf in San Francisco, USA.

The method used to load the bunkers was almost as antiquated as the ship herself. The hulk had been dis-masted and had all her rigging stripped, apart from the two lower main masts, each fitted with a swinging derrick. These were used for lifting the baskets of coal, and her steam winches were powered by a donkey boiler mounted on deck.

The Rona's crew down below would shovel coal into large baskets which would then be lifted on to a wheeled trolley that ran on a short conveyor fitted between our ship's bulwark and the bunker hatch. There was a wooden 'stop' bolted across this conveyor, and a rope tail fitted on the bottom of each basket. The trolley with basket would be pushed across the conveyor, then would hit the 'stop', and capsize the coal into the hatch. The attending man would grab the rope tail to stop the basket from disappearing into the darkness and would then toss the basket back down to the hulk for the hands below to refill it.

In these days of automation and expensive labour, it all

seems very primitive. Life was slower in the 1950's and time seemed to be cheaper. As a result, we sailors enjoyed lengthy stays in port, making local contacts and what we called "Getting our feet under the table."

The then owners of the coal hulk Rona, a well-known local shipping company called Howard Smith, eventually sold the wreck later to the National Trust for only one cent, so that restoration could commence. By that stage there were few coal burning ships left in the world, and the coal hulks were made redundant.

Once we had unloaded all of our cargo, we proceeded down the River Yarra to its mouth and the original heritage seaport area known as Williamstown, to load a full cargo of wheat for Indonesia.

My social memories of Melbourne in those days, apart from the Mission, consisted of trips to the 'pictures' and the ritual of buying an ice cream during the interval between the trailers, the news and cartoons, and the main feature. There was also a shortage of decent places to eat, and many cafes had the apparently mandated bottle of sauce full of dead flies on every table.

It was also my first experience of bigotry, mainly between Catholics and Non-conformists. This was something I had not directly experienced in Britain, probably because of the over whelming numerical predominance of Protestants. This was something of a shock to me.

23. Loading Grain in Willlamstown

Lying on the western side of the mouth of the River Yarra, where the river flows into the large expanse of Port Phillip, Williamstown is known today as a Melbourne's historic seaport. Although now simply a suburban area of Melbourne today and a place of recreation, it was once a place of ships and sailors and all the attendant industries that make up a seaport.

It was peopled by those who made their living from ships and shipping, in industries like stevedoring, ship building and repairing, dry docks, a base for tugs and Pilots, Port Officials, Customs, etc. All these items were based in Wiilliamstown, and being a sailors' town, taverns were plentifully located as were many lodging houses and brothels, plus Seamens' Missions that catered for sailors' welfare. Today many of these same buildings are popular restaurants and coffee houses.

In the early days, prior to 1874 and before the lower reaches of the River Yarra were widened by the Coode Canal, ocean going ships could not reach the new capital city of Melbourne and would anchor in the waters of Hobson's Bay and discharge their cargos and passengers into lighters, to be taken either to Williamstown or Sandridge (now Port Melbourne) on the other side of the Bay.

More expensive transport to the City was provided by early steam boats and it is said that the cost of transferring to the City in these was even more expensive than the fare from England to Australia. An old saying was "sharks don't only exist in the sea."

Gradually piers were built for visiting ships and these were serviced by a railway network to support the growing agricultural exports of the new farmlands of Victoria. The early lighthouse was converted to a Time Ball Tower, so that visiting ships could check their chronometers when the ball dropped at 1pm each day. This became redundant in 1928 with the advent of radio time signals.

A signal station was located on the harbour breakwater and each ship would receive its berthing instructions by morse-lamp.

Much has been written about the maritime history of Williamstown but suffice to say here is that it might have become the Capital of Victoria but for the lack of an adequate water supply. The city is built on hard bluestone granite which makes the drilling of wells difficult.

The quarrying of this bluestone by convict labour, who were imprisoned aboard convict ships anchored in the Bay, did provide necessary ballast for the ships sailing back to Europe in the days before sufficient exports provided an

23. Loading Grain in Williamstown

alternative. This ballast was needed for the stormy passage eastwards across the Southern Ocean, around Cape Horn, and thence to Europe. Ships requiring such ballast would signal to lighters based at the foot of Stevedore Street, hence the street's name.

The town provided easy access for ships and their cargoes of goods and migrants during the years of the Gold Rush in the 1850's. At this time the anchorage in Hobsons Bay was crowded with ships, some even deserted by gold hungry sailors. The port flourished and became a main centre for the exports of the young colony.

Up to even the early 1950's Williamstown was the major seaport for the export of wheat, later to be replaced by the speedier bulk loading conveyors of Geelong which are operating today.

Our ship, the Saint Gregory, was actually one of the last ships to load wheat at Williamstown in 1951, and this was perhaps the final chapter to close this historic shipping link in the development of Victoria. However, Williamstown, with the famous Alfred Graving Dock, remained as the centre of shipbuilding, with the Naval Dockyard constructing and servicing many of the ships that have served in the Royal Australian Navy during both world wars and peacetime, until finally privatised in 1976.

Before loading the cargo of grain, we employed a team of shipwrights whose job was to fit timber Shifting Boards and Feeders, supported by wire braces. Grain is only one step away from water, and tends to shift when a ship rolls in a seaway. To prevent this happening, shifting boards are fitted, like longitudinal bulkheads, and feeder boxes were built to keep the lower holds topped up, as the grain settled down. This job took about a week.

Loading the cargo in those days was also a slow process. Each hatch had a gang of 'stevedores, known locally as 'wharfies'. The hatch boards would be staggered, with gaps of perhaps three inches between them. The first three slings of bagged grain were used to build a platform. Once ready, slings of bags would land on the platform and be slit open to allow the grain the fall into the hold below, where it would be shovelled evenly by the workers below. Even working around the clock, it took twelve days to load the ship.

This gave us plenty of time to explore the town. I remember there were three places dedicated to sailors' welfare, the Flying Angel, the Stella Maris, and the British Sailors Society. All these places are still standing today, but have become snack bars or restaurants. In fact, Williamstown today is really a Tourist Centre and is labelled as the Historic Seaport.

Every other building along the waterfront was a tavern but now used for other purposes and Williamstown was once a Port of Entry. The Customs House was the Shipping Office and once housed the Harbour Pilots. It is now a restaurant, and the main workshop area for all the Port utilities is where the Seaworks Museum is today. The Harbour tugs and a fleet of dredgers and mud barges were also based here.

The Graving Dock in Nelson Place was built in 1870's. It was large enough to service the ships of the Royal Navy and the ships of the then Victorian State Navy. Many ships of the Royal Australian Navy were built and serviced here, but it is now unused, and all shipbuilding and repair work is gone.

Most of the seagoing facilities of Williamstown are now elsewhere, and only echoes of the past remain. While it is mainly a place of tourism and recreation with cafes and restaurants, it is the home of several yacht clubs and boat builders, with yacht chandlers and souvenir shops thrown in.

Eventually, we completed loading a full cargo of grain and then sailed for Surabaya in Indonesia.

Little did I know that I was to return later in my life to become a resident of Williamstown. It is now my turn to say "Have a good trip" to ships as they passed down the river to their worldwide destinations.

24. Loading copra in the Philippine Islands for USA

After discharging the grain in Surabaya, we went to the Philippine Islands to load copra for San Francisco, and then to be under U.S. charter for carrying armaments to the conflict in Korea.

Using Cebu, the second largest port in the Philippines, as the Port of Entry, we spent nearly three weeks moving from island to island to load bulk copra, the country's largest export. With few exceptions, the country is not wealthy, and copra is the mainstay for a huge section of the population.

Copra is the husks of coconuts, sun dried usually, and therefore both production and processing costs are low. It was the main source of income for many of the islands we loaded at. We would anchor off the island, and copra was brought out to the ship by barges, usually in those days they were ex-landing craft from the war.

It was a pleasant, peaceful time. Each of the islands visited was almost idyllic, certainly compared with the usual seaport we went to. Perhaps the poverty of the people meant a level of gratitude towards us, because by taking their copra we were helping them to survive, even if the major share of the profit would end up in the pockets of some industrialist in Manila.

Every settlement we visited had one general store, including a bar, and always run by a Chinese family. These establishments were the only sources of recreation for us, aided by Manila Rum and San Miguel beer. I can remember two such places, and I can now tell those stories.

(I remember the Copra Beetles that we also loaded at the same time, but they are part of another story told elsewhere in the book of memories.)

The Anti Huk Patrol.

I can't recall the name of this particular island — we visited so many — but it was in the heart of land disputed by communist insurgents, fighting for their independence from the central Government in Manila. They were known in those days as the Huks. They existed in jungle areas, and were sought out by regular patrols of thousands of Government troops.

Some of us were enjoying the hospitality of the local Chinese establishment, when an armoured car, manned by an officer and four soldiers pulled up outside. These were Government soldiers on an anti-Huk patrol. They were hot and thirsty and decided that their duty could pause while they took a little cold refreshment.

By this time we had reached a gregarious state, and became very friendly with this military group. I remember sharing addresses with the young officer in particular, and we all became great chums, singing songs and generally enjoying the evening together.

Eventually the time came when our new friends decided that they should resume their patrol, and warmed by the new friendship and perhaps by the Manila Rum, I asked if I could come with them.

I was told that I would be welcome, but that there was no room within the armoured car and that I would have to sit outside, by the gun turret. I accepted the invitation, and with a final "whoop" we were off, driving into the night and into the jungle.

I was fascinated by all this, the jungle illuminated by the headlights, the night sounds of the forest, the overhanging trees, and the odd wild animal caught napping by our sudden appearance. It was certainly fascinating.... at first — until the alcoholic sedation started to wear off. It was then I realised that I was a sitting duck, sitting outside the armour, and would be the first to be shot at if we ran into any trouble.

It was not so funny from that point on, and by the time we arrived back at the village I was a nervous wreck. The whole exercise was interesting, but I was very relieved and glad to be back on board the ship, and in the safety of my bunk.

The Smith and Wesson Quickstep. !

It all happened while we were loading copra from barges while anchored off the small island of St.Pedro di Macoris, one of many islands in the Philippines that we visited. We were there for about three days, until we shifted to another island.

It so happened that during lunch on the last day, I had been involved in a discussion with the Third Officer on the subject of how to settle a dispute.

"Give them a good punch in the face, that will solve any argument," said the rather aggressive Third Mate whose name was John. "That's the way we fix things in Glasgow!"

"Oh, I know that's how you would settle things in Scotland," I answered, "But I believe that there is a better way. If you smile and act in a gentle, non-belligerent manner, you can talk your way eventually out of any situation," ..... And so on and so on. Those in the saloon listened to the two of us arguing endlessly but without any conclusion, until it was time to go back to work.

The daylight faded, the evening meal was served, and plans were laid by those not on duty to spend the evening ashore. There was not much entertainment that this small settlement could offer, and many of the Officers decided to stay on board. However, four of us decided that a few hours spent at the small Chinese trader's place, drinking the local Manila rum, would be a break from our usual ship routine.

So off we went. This meant clinging to an empty cargo

24. Loading copra in the Philippine Islands for USA

net and being lowered to the deck of the now empty barge alongside, then being ferried to the local pier. The store was nearby, and we were encouraged on the way by the grins and friendly gestures of the local people.

The evening turned out much as expected, but I guess the effects of the alcohol consumed generated the usual desires felt by young men, and particularly young sailors deprived of female company, and in the end the Chinese bar keeper was questioned about other activities available in the village.

"Where are all the girls?" "There must be some life somewhere. Is there no dance hall or anything?" The questions kept being asked, and eventually we were told that if we followed a track to the water's edge, we would find a timber walkway, and at the end there was a shack that was used as a dance hall. It was equipped with an ancient record player, and a cheap form of alcohol was served. We drank our drinks and went exploring.

I believe that had we not been emboldened by the rum, we would not have undertaken this venture. The route was frightening and very lonely, and felt so very threatening in the dark. Eventually, the sounds of a scratchy record player became the bait we needed to continue, and finally the dim lights of the shack appeared through the jungle mists.

The good nature of us seafarers, the acts of friendship, and our laughter, saw us through, and we settled down in our dubious surroundings. Looking around we saw a mixed group of about twenty, all either suffering from drugs or drink but in the main not a particularly wholesome group.

In the dim light I saw one youngish looking female, who seemed to be a cut above the others, so I decided that at least I would ask her to dance. I approached her, and although there was no mutual language, the understanding was clear, and next minute the two of us were cavorting around the dance floor and having a great flirtatious time. I felt that I was making progress.

Suddenly, there was a change of atmosphere. Our dancing had been interrupted by the biggest Philipino man I had ever seen and who was obviously the boyfriend of this girl. He jumped between us, and made it obvious that he objected to my flirtations with his girlfriend by pointing a pearl handled revolver at me.

This was a new experience and I was paralysed. In fact I think we were all stunned by this event, and we suddenly became aware of the hostility of our surroundings. I for one was afraid for my own safety in this dubious place.

The whole place became silent and we could feel the tension rising. Suddenly a Scottish voice boomed out across the hall. "Talk your way out of that one, Charley," shouted John, "See if those fancy ideas of yours for making peace really work this time."

I must admit that afterwards I realised that if I had I not been so drunk I would have been too afraid to do anything, but instead I smiled and I bravely said to this mad looking

24. Loading copra in the Philippine Islands for USA

person threatening me, "That's a good looking gun. Could I have a closer look at it?"

To my amazement, the evil looking man handed me the gun.

Here I was, with the hot gun in my hot little hand. I had never handled a revolver before in my life and I really did not know what to do with it, so after pretending a close inspection I handed the gun back to the gunman, shook his hand, and introduced myself.

I then brought him and the girl to our table and introduced all the rest of the gang from the ship. John bought our new friends a drink and later even invited them down to visit the ship the next day, knowing we were due to sail by then.

The ice was broken, thank God. We bought drinks all round, but it still seemed wise to leave soon afterwards, glad we were safe and sound, and we scurried back to the security of our ship.

What a story we would tell on board the next day, but if the truth was known, we were glad to be alive and able to tell it.

Eventually, and with a full cargo of copra and attendant beetles, we sailed for San Francisco, to load munitions for the war in Korea.

Note. I have written about these copra beetles, under the heading of 'Copra Bugs' in a chapter called 'The Maritime Menagerie.' — all about the various non-human 'shipmates'

I sailed with on different ships over the years that I spent at sea.

25. Loading for Korean War

Our introduction to the West Coast of the United States was with a cargo of copra (and copra beetles) loaded in many different islands in the Philippines for San Francisco. There we came under charter to an American company for two trips with armaments for the war in Korea.

We loaded these arms in San Francisco itself, across in Alameda, in Long Beach, and in San Diego, and I have many both fond and sad memories of each of those places, each crowded with young Americans recruited for the conflict and determined to enjoy life before being shipped out — perhaps to die.

In San Francisco I remember taking our Chinese bosun to a dentist who advertised himself as 'Painless Parker'.

We were entertained there by the family of the British Consul, and I enjoyed my first Thanksgiving Day at their house, playing with electric trains given to their son. Their daughters took us to the City's famous Flower Show, always a top annual event. There I can remember listening to bagpipes played by a piper dressed in full highland regalia. He was as black as the Ace of Spades, and at that time it seemed incongruous.

In Alameda I met the realities of the American colour bar that existed at that time. It happened after I was invited to a party by some coloured sailors that I had met in a bar. We piled into a taxi, but I was told to lie on the floor because if a white man was seen in the company of dark people, a riot might start. It all seemed so wrong, because these young coloured men were fighting for the U.S.

In Long Beach, the seaport for Los Angeles, many happy evenings were spent at what was then known as 'the Pike', an area of amusement arcades and speakeasy bars, but what has now become a large Marina. There was one Bar we adopted called the Silver Dollar and their juke box was a phone link to a central music base. Our voices gave us away, and the operators would greet us with exaggerated 'Limey' accents. This was a time of hits by Doris Day, Nat King Cole, and the like.

This bar had printed beer mats, and I can remember the poem printed on these to this day;

Drunk is he who on the floor
Prostrate lies, and cannot rise.
But not drunk is he, who from the floor
Can rise again and drink some more.

Two U.S. sailors that I met one evening spent some happy time at this bar teaching each other the rudiments of both Gridiron Football and Rugby, using a sugar shaker as the ball, until play was halted by the bar manager. Later, I was taken back to their ship, a U.S. destroyer, called by them a Can and after coffee and a tour of the ship, I was put to bed in one of their mess decks. I did not know it, but my hosts had hung a sign "DUTY COOK" over my bunk. After barely an hours sleep, I was rudely awakened by a sentry who was very surprised to find a Limey stowaway in the bed. My British voice gave me away when I (very politely) asked him to leave me in peace. Later, breakfast was an exercise in American democracy.

It is said that one should never return to a place because it will not seem the same. I have returned to these Californian cities many times in my later business life, but never did they seemed the same, when I compared them to the wonderful friendship and happy times we had enjoyed during our stays during the time of our two voyages to Korea.

Auckland and Rangitoto Island

26. Auckland to Liverpool

To Nauru; Phosphate for New Zealand and thence to Europe

We sailed light ship i.e. without cargo and in ballast from Japan to Nauru, to load phosphate for Auckland, and then to load in various New Zealand ports for Alexandria, Genoa, and Liverpool.

I was glad to be visiting Auckland, because it was the only place in Australasia that I had relatives — my mother's sister Helen lived there. She had married a Kiwi soldier after the first World War and emigrated at that time. Aunt Helen was several years older than mother. She had not had any children and had been a widow for some years at that time. She was not wealthy and lived on the North Shore in a place called Mairangi Bay. Before the bridge was built across the harbour, this journey entailed a ferry from the City, then a long bus ride through early settlements.

My first memories of the city of Auckland are somewhat sketchy, for I spent most of my time there with my Aunt, who by this time was quite old and frail. My first impressions were therefore of a simple and unsophisticated life.

It was later, after many visits with New Zealand Shipping Company that led me to a fondness of the country and its people and a decision to live there.

An interesting features were the local air connections. Internationally, the airline was called TEAL, or Trans Empire Airways Limited, and in the early 1950's used flying boats to Sydney and London, and a very expensive mode of travel. Most people went by sea.

An interesting feature was the use of the main shipping channel as the flight path for these flying boats, and this had to be cleared of ships and boats at the times of aircraft movement.

We discharged the whole cargo of phosphate in Auckland, and then loaded there a cargo of wool, hides, and tallow, and then at other NZ ports — Napier, Wellington, Lyttelton, and Bluff, for discharge at Alexandria, Genoa, and Liverpool.

Once we completed loading at Bluff we were homeward bound, though it was a long voyage via the Great Circle trip to Western Australia and then through Suez to Italy and the UK.

Passing south of Tasmania into the Southern Ocean we encountered very rough weather and butted into head seas all the way to Fremantle. With slow progress against storm after storm, we were forced into the beautiful port of Albany for emergency coal bunkers before rounding Cape Leeuin, on the SW corner of Australia.

This was my only time to visit Albany, which was at

the time the home of Australia's whaling industry, and remembered as the assembly port for the departure of the Australian troops heading for conflict in Europe. It is a magnificent harbour, and has not reached its potential because of the remoteness of that part of Australia.

When we sailed from Albany, we encountered a further succession of storms and our slow progress around Cape Leeuwin had been headlined by the Perth newspapers and on arrival at Fremantle the journalists were disappointed to find that the only damage sustained was to some of the crockery broken when the steward dropped a tray.

The rest of the trip to UK was pretty usual with mainly fine weather even in the Mediterranean Sea and the Bay of Biscay. The only thing worthy of mention was the mess the labourers in Alexandria made by trying to lift the tallow from storm damaged casks by means of rope slings. These acted like cheese cutters and the tallow was spread far and wide in a terrible sticky mess.

Our visit to Genoa was very brief, but in one evening ashore we found our visit coincided with that of the U.S. Fleet, which meant that prices on all sorts of refreshments virtually doubled.

The bar that we went to was the scene of a wild brawl involving U.S. sailors and local young men, probably over the local girls. We did not get involved and barricaded ourselves into a corner of the room and were simply spectators. The melee was broken up by the arrival of USN

Military police, who lashed out indiscriminately with their night sticks, while we were able to get on with our entertainment of the local lasses.

Discharge and part loading in Liverpool meant some brief Leave and time spent with my brother John. It was a happy time, with friendly banter between the RN and the MN. It was actually the last time I saw him before he was tragically lost in the submarine HMS Affray months later.

27. The Loss Of HMS Affray

This occurred in April 1951, and I was then a Cadet aboard a British ship, the "Saint Gregory". We had finished discharging cargo from New Zealand in Liverpool and were bound for Hamburg in Germany where, as part of wartime reparations, the ship was to undergo conversion from coal fired boilers to those heated by oil fuel.

It was a clear and sunny Monday morning, and we were somewhere north of Scotland when I was summoned to the Bridge, to be met by a sombre looking Captain holding a signal message, and greeted with the words "I have just received this message from your Father, asking me to tell you that your brother John is aboard the submarine "Affray" which has failed to send a routine signal on surfacing this morning, and is posted as missing."

This was a shock to me though, in truth, John and I were not all that close. He was five years older than me and had entered the RN at seventeen when I was only twelve years old. Five years age difference is a lifetime when one is a child. Furthermore, I had been doomed to following in his footsteps and had become tired of being told "you are not as good as your brother was". That's one of the reasons for breaking the pattern by joining the Merchant Navy where as he was in the RN. He had enjoyed odd leaves at home, but these times were spent mainly with the girl he eventually married — they had enjoyed their first wedding anniversary just the day before the Affray sailed on that fateful trip. Since I started my apprenticeship at sea, aged sixteen, our leaves never coincided.

John had obtained his first "ring" as a Sub-Lieutenant and served board "Dido" and "Dunkirk", while I was on long voyages mainly in the Far East, and I actually spent more time at sea than he had in merely a couple of years. It was not until the New Year in 1951 that we spent some time together, the first occasion in nearly five years. He and his wife, June, had just moved into a flat at Weymouth, and I was able to spend a couple of days with them.

Just prior to this time, John had been promoted as a full Lieutenant Engineer, and was serving aboard HMS Vanguard, the last of the RN capital ships. He resented that he spent most of his time providing ice for the ship's cocktail parties and consequently he volunteered for service in submarines. This fateful last voyage aboard HMS Affray was the culmination of his training program

The Saint Gregory arrived in Hamburg on the Monday evening, and the German agents worked hard to make sure that I was able to be on the Hook of Holland to Harwich Ferry on the Tuesday night. They were so wonderful and

27. The Loss Of HMS Affray

sympathetic, and I shall never forget their kindness.

This was all a bit of a shock to me. I had been through the Blitz in London and had been machine-gunned in the streets by German fighters. As a result, I was brought up to believe "the only good German was a dead German'. How we learn differently as life goes on.

I arrived home on the Wednesday to find my parents distraught, with the search for the missing submarine still going on. John's wife June had travelled from Weymouth to give comfort to my Mother in the traditional spirit of "They also serve, who only wait at home".

We did nothing but listen for good news, and to hope and pray. No such message came and, on the Saturday, it was decided that all hope was gone, and the 95 officers and men were all pronounced dead. My employers, Saint Line, granted me two weeks compassionate leave, and then I re-joined the ship in Hamburg, later to sail for Ghent in Belgium and to load for the States.

We learnt later that the hull of the "Affray" was found about three months later but was in water too deep for salvage. Identification of the wreck was by the first ever use of underwater television.

The site was to be marked by wreaths, cast from Royal Navy ships by relatives of those that perished, including my parents. My eldest son was given the same names as my brother — John Monkton Treleaven, and he was actually born on the anniversary of the Affray's loss. I remember my mother saying at the time "John has come back'. She had aged many years as a result of John's loss, and had trouble accepting the fact that her son was dead. She had actually turned to Spiritualism because of this.

Many years later, I took my Australian family for a visit to Portsmouth in UK where we visited the chapel at HMS Dolphin, which was the Base of the British submarine fleet at the time. We saw the memorial to those that were lost aboard the "Affray", with their names listed. It was a moving moment.

Sometime later, a monument was erected at the entrance to Portsmouth Harbour to commemorate HMS Affray and her crew. The unveiling ceremony was attended by my brother's widow, June, and my children Nicholas and Wendy.

28. Ghent — What is in a Name.

The recent explosion in Lebanon has made me remember an incident once experienced in Ghent, Belgium In 1952, aboard the "Saint Gregory". I was a cadet at the time.

We had sailed from Hamburg to load for Newport News in the USA. In actual fact we were the largest ship ever to visit the Port of Ghent to that time, and I remember that we went through the port's lock with only inches to spare. (This led to subsequent leakage in mid- Atlantic, but that is another story.)

Memories of the chemical explosion that had occurred in 1947 in Texas City were still fresh. This was caused by an ammonium nitrate explosion, similar to the big one in Lebanon this week. It happened when the cargo loaded aboard a French ship went on fire and then exploded. This enormous explosion resulted in the deaths of up to 600 people, with over 6000 injured, and wiped out most of the City of Galveston. An anchor and part-propeller from the French ship were found about one mile away.

Aboard our ship, the word went out that we were to load 9,500 tons of ammonium nitrate, and that there would be no smoking aboard. Severe anti-fire restrictions were imposed. All of us in charge of loading cargo were told to watch the wharf labourers carefully, and to make sure that they complied with these strict rules.

All of us were very nervous when loading commenced, and to my horror, I found a man lighting a cigarette on deck. I rushed up to him, and sternly admonished him. I was amazed at his laughter, and especially when he grabbed a handful of the cargo and put a match to it. By this time, I was half way down the deck in panic.

But nothing happened. The match went out, and only the laughter remained.

It was then discovered that we were actually loading Ammonium Sulphate, which is quite inert, and not the dangerous Ammonium Nitrate we had previously been warned about.

It was just another moment to remember from my years at sea.

29. Ghent to Newport News, & Puerto Rico.

The departure from Ghent and the narrowness of the harbour lock there, led to a later problem that only came to light when we were half way across the Atlantic Ocean.

The carpenter reported that the routine soundings of the bilges in No.2 Hold were showing signs leakage, by water gathering in the bilges. Inspection later showed that some rivets had been sheered off, probably in the lock at Ghent, but only the worsening weather had caused the damage to become apparent.

Temporary repair could be achieved by a cement box fitted internally over the holes, but to achieve this, the cargo of ammonium sulphate would need to be shovelled clear of the area.. What a great job for the cadets!

The atmosphere in the hold was quite putrid and thick, but not a thought was given that the air might have been poisonous. Fortunately it was not — well, at least I'm still alive after all these years. However, every time the ship rolled, the cargo that had been removed would shift back again, so this had to be solved. The use of dunnage (timber) to build a barrier was used and thus the cargo was held clear of the ship's side.

The job took nearly all day, and then we helped the ship's carpenter to build the cement box between the frames. He mixed the cement with plenty of bi-carb to make it dry quickly. It thus all held together until we arrived in USA, where proper repairs could be made.

The Port of Newport News is also the largest U.S. naval base on the Atlantic coast. It is prominent in the history of the War of Independence, and recently what is thought to be the remains of Cook's ship "Endeavour" were found there. This was among the wrecks of ships sunk to block the passage into the Sound.

The "Endeavour" after Cook's first voyage to the South Pacific, had an interesting career with the Royal Navy. She became a transport ship, and among other experiences she had been used to evacuate the garrison of the Falkland Islands, and then later to take British troops as reinforcements for the war fought against the Argentine.

Newport is also the home of the Mariner's Museum, one of many that lie along the East Coast of the United States. Certainly, the U.S. is proud of its maritime history and the traditions that have been born, somewhat in contrast to Australia.

One of the salient features of this Museum was the evidence that America was first discovered by the Vikings, well before Christopher Columbus crossed the Atlantic. A feature of this museum was a striking statue of Leif Eriksson, the Viking who is thought to be the first European to land in the New World, and there are the remains in Newfoundland of a Viking village, said to have been built in about 1000 AD.

Ever since 1964, America holds Leif Eriksson Day on October 9th each year. Most Americans have never understood the reason for this celebration. Everybody has heard of Columbus, but who was this other fellow?

Visit to San Juan — Porto Rico and the Dominican Republic.

Part of our cargo from Ghent was for San Juan, on the island of Porto Rico, which is actually ruled as part of the USA ever since it was ceded to them at the turn-of the century following the American-Spanish war.

Those of us aboard were not aware of this, and we arrived off the port with the Porto Rican flag flying as a curtesy flag. We were greeted by an American military flying boat who warned us by loud hailer to "remove that rebel flag or we will sink you." The flag was immediately replaced with the "Old Glory", the Stars and Stripes. We found later that the question of local independence was a touchy subject.

This was part of my only trip to the West Indies. Because we had only a small part-cargo for San Juan, we were not there long enough to explore it very much. That was a pity, because the place has a very interesting past and an equally fascinating library of mixed architecture. The island was settled by the Spanish very soon after the second voyage of Columbus, and thereafter the British and French and even pirates, had made unsuccessful attempts to take possession.

On the one evening we went ashore I can remember our eccentric Radio Officer taking over a street protest meeting and by speaking very forcibly, he sought to persuade the local people to join the movement for self-rule, with independence from the United States.

Being from the Irish Republic he was well versed in the slogans of freedom. I remember the crowd's fervour reaching a pitch, forcing us to run and to escape from the attention of the American police. We ran fast back to our ship to avoid being arrested as 'agents provocateur', not realising the seriousness of the situation. To us it was just a huge joke.

Fortunately we sailed early the next day for the Dominican Republic to load sugar for Glasgow and there were never any repercussions.

30. Loading sugar in The Dominican Republic

The voyage in ballast to the loading port in the Dominican Republic, San Pedro, was only short, and the weather was picture-book calm. The country shares an island with Haiti, and is the dominant partner by its size, though economically it is the probably the poorest Nation in the whole West Indies — at that time anyway.

When we arrived, the contrast between the opulence of San Juan and the abject poverty of this place was obvious and dramatic. The people were downcast and oppressed and obviously very poor, the streets were unsealed, and everything was unpainted and dirty. This was in the early 1950's but I doubt if it has changed much.

We learnt that the country had been ransacked for years by its Dictator, Rafael Trujillo, and the country was run as a police state. Corruption was rife at all levels, and even though Trujillo was assassinated in 1961, the corruption seemed too systemic to ever be stopped. (The story of Trujillo's reign and the history of the Dominican Republic is fascinating, even nearly unbelievable, reading.)

The loading of sugar was fairly uneventful, though we were kept busy in chasing thieves in every corner of the ship. The people would take anything. We also observed that the wharf labourers used urine as a handy disinfectant in the event of a wound — at least it was cheap and effective, even though the natural brown sugar was sometimes sprayed as well. I still think of that every time I look for the sugar bowl. We made a joke about us being British and that we only used refined sugar

There was another British ship loading sugar in port there. She was the M.V. "La Sierra" one of Beris Mark's Line from Liverpool, crewed, I am afraid, by the dregs of that seaport. Some of their sailors had discovered that they could enjoy the company of the local 'prostitutes' in return for articles of clothing, even in the absence of any money. Imagine what they could achieve for just a pair of old socks.

The evening before that ship sailed for the UK, the 'Saint Gregory' was visited by scantily clad sailors, bludging any clothes in preparation for a return to the English winter, though I think personal warmth was actually the least of their later physical problems.

It took us about a week to load a full cargo of sugar. The cargo was mainly from split bags, with a layer of bagged sugar on top to provide stability.

With our off-duty time spent swimming and boating, enjoying plenty of sunshine and smooth white sandy beaches, and with other times spent socializing with the

30. Loading sugar in The Dominican Republic

more decent local citizens over a few local rums, it was for us a pleasant enough spot, though not a place we would ever want to live.

With some regret we eventually sailed for Glasgow in the U.K., facing an awful winter in the North Atlantic, and cold in Liverpool. Life at sea is like the famous Parson's egg — good and bad in places — and one learns to endure anything the elements throw at you.

Harbour and city of Marmagoa.

31. At Portuguese Marmagoa.

"We are going Home" This thrilling news was given to us by Sparks — the Radio Officer — after the Captain told him to do so.

In 1953, the ship "Saint Gregory" had been trading for eighteen months all over the world on a voyage typical of a British 'tramp' ship at that time. It seemed like we would never see the UK again. We had a Chinese crew, with only fourteen British officers, including the Captain and four Cadets. At sea, with some of us on Watches, and others sleeping, it was difficult to find players for a four handed game of cards.

The actual homecoming was still a long way off. At that time we were loading rice in Bangkok for India, and after that we were to load coal in Calcutta for Melbourne, and then carry grain from Port Lincoln in South Australia, to Bombay in India. After that trip we were to go "light ship" to Marmagoa on the West Coast of India to load iron ore for Rotterdam in Holland. This was still not the UK, but Northern European ports were classed as Home Ports and those entitled could be "paid off" there and to go to UK on leave.

On arrival in Rotterdam, I would obtain a release from my four years indentures as a Cadet. I would be leaving the ship to sit for my Second Mate's Certificate of Competency and this meant that I could look forward to perhaps three months at home while studying. The sea had stolen my youthful years, and I was determined to make up for lost time.

At this time, Goa was still a Portuguese Colony, a situation going back in history, to when the Portuguese had trading bases and Colonies throughout Asia, Africa, and India. Sri Lanka, then still called Ceylon, was one such trading base, like Goa, as early as the sixteenth century until taken over, first by the Dutch, and then by Britain in 1815. Goa was eventually taken over by the Indians just after we were there and today it is an important centre for commerce and tourism. Its main British connection in the past was that the Liner company, P & O, recruited many of their stewards in Goa.

We eventually arrived in Goa, navigated a narrow harbour entrance and anchored in an inner bay, which was a well sheltered and provided a quite extensive harbour. There were a couple of other ships anchored, and soon we were surrounded by a series of small craft, to fit our derricks with mechanical grabs for the purpose of loading the iron ore. The cargo would be brought out to us by barges, and loaded with these grabs. The schedule was that we would load around the clock and lift about ten thousand tons of ore in ten days.

31. At Portuguese Marmagoa.

Iron ore, unlike a grain cargo has a safe 'angle of rest' which means it can be dumped into the holds, and as long as it is spread fairly evenly, there is little danger of it shifting, no matter how much a ship rolls around in bad weather. This meant that the ship's Officers had a fairly relaxing time on cargo watch — and therefore able to make the most of this being a duty free port, — alcohol was very inexpensive, with nice beaches and attractive young ladies.

We loaded about 80% of the cargo in the lower hold, and then fitted the 'tween deck hatches, and carried the balance of ore spread out in the upper 'tween decks. This was done because iron ore is a heavy, high density material, and if all the weight was carried low in the ship, the forces of gravity would cause the ship to roll very fast and uncomfortably, even by repute in some cases, rolling the masts out! Rotterdam was far away, and the infamous Bay of Biscay lay ahead.

Morma Goa was an interesting study for onshore and offshore breezes. The Cadets had to take the Captain ashore in a lifeboat, supposedly for business, but in reality to have lunch and enjoy the local hospitality. Being within a land locked harbour, we found that by leaving the ship by about ten in the morning, we could catch the last of the night 'offshore' breeze, and actually sail the boat to the pier. We would then tie up waiting for the Captain's call, to return to the ship.

In the afternoon, after two o'clock, we could sail back to the ship using the 'onshore' breeze, and therefore not having to rely on the very unreliable lifeboat engine. Otherwise, it was a long row back to the ship.

The German Spy Ships.

At the time of our visit, the authorities were blasting the wrecks of three German ships which had been interned by the Portuguese during World War 2. Even though the ships were interned in a neutral place, British intelligence discovered that one of the German ships had a hidden radio transmitter, and was transmitting messages from Indian spies giving details about allied ships leaving nearby Bombay to German submarines offshore, resulting in unsustainable ship losses and their valuable cargoes.

This posed a quandary for the British because Goa was Portuguese territory. They could not take direct action because that would cause a breach of neutrality, and endanger the agreed use by allied planes of airfields in the Azores Islands in the Atlantic. The local Portuguese Goanese authorities denied that anything was happening, and refused to search the ships for the secret radio.

The British devised a cunning plot. In Calcutta, there was a long established military club, "The Calcutta Light Horse", retaining mainly elderly British servicemen, now too old to take part actively in the current conflict. These men, unfit and paunchy, were sworn to secrecy, made to do some toughening up exercises to the amazement of their wives, then

31. At Portuguese Marmagoa.

given training in explosives and modern weapons, and sent on a mission to destroy the German ships. This is a true story.

The British Consul in Goa was in on the act and bribed the local brothel madams to offer a free night to the German sailors, thus reducing the number of crew on each ship during the attack. The British purchased an old dredger in Calcutta and sailed it round to the vicinity of Goa, to take on the Boarding Party. These men had pretended to be on recreational leave in Goa. The whole exercise was a great success and the hidden radio was destroyed, the ships were sunk, and casualties on either side were light.

In 1980 this whole story was the subject of a book called "Boarding Party" and a successful movie called "The Sea Wolves" which had a huge cast of well-known actors. As stated — this was a true story.

During our visit, every afternoon at about three o'clock the Portuguese would detonate charges which were laid to destroy the wrecks. We would take a party of our Chinese crew in another of our lifeboats to compete with the local Indians in picking up some of the resultant stunned or dead fish. The Battle of Trafalgar was as nothing compared to this scrum every afternoon.

Under Fire

We eventually completed loading and were due to sail early next day for Rotterdam. After squaring up the ship and making her ready for sea, about eight of us went ashore to celebrate, and to purchase duty free grog to take home. This was so cheap — a bottle of genuine Drambuie whisky liquor would cost only about 75 cents — an opportunity not be missed.

On the way back to the pier where our lifeboat was tied up, a Portuguese policeman tried to make us pay an "exit tax" on our parcels of drinks. Our Third Mate, a wild Scotsman called John, and never one to trifle with, told us all to get back aboard our boat quickly, while he kept the policeman talking. Eventually John came running to join us with the instructions to move and "row like hell". John had apparently exercised some Glasgow diplomacy and laid out our friendly policeman with a Scottish left hook.

We were about two hundred yards from the pier when we came under revolver fire and a hail of bullets. I can remember making myself as small as possible, and using the bulk of the Fourth Engineer as shelter. This was my first experience of actually being under fire.

All this time we were rowing as hard as possible, and eventually we arrived back to our ship, with no wounds, and with our special parcels of cheap drinks. We were exhausted, but this same Fourth Engineer was not even puffed. It turned out that while the rest of us were rowing ourselves silly and pulling on those heavy oars, he had grabbed the boat hook without noticing in the dark that it was not an oar. That was his story anyway — he even

31. At Portuguese Marmagoa.

expressed how easy he found that trip.

For some reason, the Authorities did not follow any of this up, which surprised us. Perhaps there was no exit tax and the policeman was just trying to gain a little extra money, or perhaps they were not sure which ship in the harbour we came from. Anyway, there were no repercussions and we sailed early the next morning for Rotterdam.

City of Bombay.

32. Morma Goa to Rotterdam

It was a long voyage from Morma Goa to Rotterdam. Across the Indian Ocean, then taking on coal bunkers at Aden, and through the Red Sea to the Suez Canal. In late November it was the onset of winter in Europe. Arrival at Suez at this time of year would see us wearing our white tropical uniforms, but during the passage of the Canal the temperature would drop and we would change into winter uniforms. By the time we sailed from Port Said into a stormy Mediterranean, we were wrapped in our winter 'blue' uniforms and all our warmest sweaters.

As our ship passed Europa Point at Gibraltar we entered the last leg of our long voyage. We knew that we still had to pass through the dreaded Bay of Biscay to enter the English Channel. The Bay was to live up to its reputation, and soon after passing Point Trafalgar we received a storm warning, and what a storm it turned out to be.

Our radio auto-alarm system alerted us to the first of the casualties. An American freighter, the "Flying Enterprise" was a victim of shifting cargo, and was lying with a list of over 60 degrees, and in danger of sinking. A British freighter

Wreck of 'Flying Enterprise".

had rescued all the crew except the Master, Captain Larsen, who remained aboard the hulk for insurance purposes. The ship was still afloat, like a half tide rock. The captain was eventually joined by the First Mate of salvage tug "Turmoil", in what became known as "Darcy's Leap" and there exists today a wonderful photograph of the Captain and Darcy walking down the ship's funnel to be rescued just before the ship finally capsized.

    We ourselves were in trouble. Our steam powered steering engine broke down, and left us drifting, broadside to mountainous seas and rolling heavily. While we were in this situation, with huge green waves crashing over the ship, our Number Two hatch was stove in, allowing water

32. Morma Goa to Rotterdam

to enter the hold and endangering our very survival. The Master handled the ship well, and by going slowly astern and without any steering, he brought the ship's stern into the wind, giving some respite to those of us working on the foredeck. This allowed us to repair the damage, and to spread spare tarpaulins.

At the same time, the Engineers fixed the steering gear, and we were able to adopt a more usual and comfortable "hove to" position, but still unable to make headway against the storm. This was when we picked up a distress call from a British ship, the "Tressillion", one of the Haynes Line ships, bound from Vancouver to Liverpool with grain. In the storm, her shifting boards had carried away, the grain cargo had shifted, and she was heavily listed. It was soon after her distress call that the ship capsized, with quite a heavy loss of life. Although fairly close, we could do nothing to help.

We weathered the storm, and made our way into the English Channel. There is a strange disease that affects British sailors and has been well known for years. It is called "The Channels." This makes men start to think of getting home and being with loved ones. Sleeping and eating become difficult, and they seem to be a little crazy because of the excitement of home coming. After a long voyage of nearly two years this certainly affected a lot of us.

It had been calculated that we would arrive in Rotterdam early on 22rd December, and with good luck having a quick "sign off" we would be home for Christmas. The Engineers were given every bit of encouragement to get the extra half knot from the engines to make this possible.

Alas, it was not to be! We arrived about lunchtime on the 22nd to find that the British Consul, the only man who could sign us off, had gone on Leave, and would not be back until the 27th December. You can guess the rather coarse names we called him. However, we enjoyed great hospitality from the Dutch people, and we spent one of the best Christmas days that I can remember when we Cadets were adopted by some of the City's Burghers and their families.

We were "paid off" on the 27th December, caught the Hook to Harwich ferry that afternoon, and spent a raucous night aboard, arriving at Harwich the next morning. Without the fuss of armoured vans (as would happen these days) an inconspicuous character met us on the wharf. He wore a long raincoat, which was lined with several pockets on the inside, and each pocket held the money due to each of us. Once paid, we made our unemotional farewells and went our own way to our families. A typically low key end to a typical long voyage.

I can remember arriving home on that Friday evening. My mother drowned me with hugs and kisses, so excited to have her 'little boy' home, not just for a short leave but for perhaps three months while I was studying. It had been a long voyage, and in truth I had gone away as a boy, and came home a man.

32. Morma Goa to Rotterdam

I spent a happy weekend with family and friends, to be disrupted by a phone call from the Saint Line office early on the Monday morning. The manager's voice said "We have the "Cape St David" loading in London for Le Havre and due to sail on Wednesday. We need a third mate urgently. Would you be willing to help us out for a few days as an uncertificated officer?"

My mother was tearful when I broke the news that I would be leaving again so soon, and that a taxi would pick me up in an hour or so. In those days people has a strong sense of loyalty, and I could not even consider refusing to do the trip.

As it turned out, at Le Havre I was "shanghaied" into a quick trip to Matardi in the Belgian Congo, so the "few days" became something like nearly three months. At least on my return, England was approaching spring and I would not have to endure the climatical abomination of an English winter.

As a result of this experience I decided that after I passed my examination, I would seek employment with a "liner" company, whose ships were on fixed runs, and doing voyages of a more defined duration. I was confident that the choice of employment would be mine, because in 1953 most of the British shipping companies were still rebuilding their fleets and making good the losses suffered during the War. Consequently they were desperately short of qualified officers and jobs were easy to find.

The story of job seeking in Leadenhall Street in the City of London is told within Chapter 32.

33. The Unexpected trip to Matardi, Belgian Congo.

I arrived home on that Friday evening from Rotterdam, having being away for nearly two years. My mother drowned me with hugs and kisses, so excited to have her 'little boy' home, not just for a short leave but for perhaps three months while I was studying. It had been a long voyage, tramping all over the world, and in truth I had gone away as a boy, and came home as a man of nearly 21 years old. The sea had stolen much of my youth and I was determined to win some of it back.

I spent a happy weekend with family and friends, to be disrupted by a phone call from the Saint Line office early on the Monday morning. The manager's voice said "We have the "Cape St. David" loading in London for Le Havre and due to sail on Wednesday. We need a Third Mate urgently. Would you be willing to help us out for a few days as an uncertificated officer for the trip to Le Havre?" There was no doubt about my decision, and even my mother's tears did not deter me. It was not from fear of any future unemployment, nor from fear of losing Study Pay because we did not get any in those days. It was just the belief to do the right thing.

We were only in Le Havre a short time, (in sailors' language only a 'Dog Watch'.) The only place I had visited in France before was Marseilles in the south, and Le Havre did not seem much of an improvement. It was here that I was asked to stay for the round trip to discharge the explosives in Dakar, and then to proceed to Matardi, in the Belgian Congo, to load for Rotterdam.

Therefore, the original "few days" became something like three months. At least the money earnt as Third Mate, even at the princely sum of twenty eight pounds per month, would help subsidise the meagre unemployment Dole which is all I could look forward to while studying. In any case on my return, England would be in summer and I would avoid the climatical abomination of an English winter.

The short stay in Le Havre has few memories, and the neither has the voyage off West Africa or the short time discharging in Dakar.

We went in ballast to the Congo where the fast flowing Congo River dominates the scene. The port of Matardi lies about sixty kilometres up-stream from the mouth. If you read the story of this Belgian colony you will find that it really was the property of King Leopold, not a true Colony, and held only to increase the royal wealth. Consequently, there was little done for the welfare of the Congolese, or increase their standard of living. In Matardi itself, a

33. The Unexpected trip to Matardi, Belgian Congo.

strict curfew was in place so that the comfort of the white Belgians was not disturbed. It was not surprising that in later years, the Congolese people won their independence by a bloody and fierce revolution.

However for us, the voyage up the river was exciting, and at one particular bend called the 'Devil's Cauldron' the flow is extreme between high cliffs. Our low powered steamship could barely make headway against the stream and the Bridge had constantly to ask for a few more revolutions from the overworked engines. Off all the west coast of Africa the electrical storms during the evening are spectacular, and the heat and humidity will never be forgotten. It was not called "The white man's grave" for nothing.

The Port of Matardi was serviced by passenger ships of the Elder Dempster Line, and some happy moments were spent aboard their ship, the 'Accra'. The Second Engineer had discovered that the pipe that supplied cold beer to the passengers' bar actually ran through his wardrobe. A little plumbing was all that was needed. When she sailed, the Belgian ship 'Leopoldville' took over the provision of refreshment and air-conditioned relief for those of us who were off duty.

We were ten days loading, and then sailed with a full cargo of iron ore for Rotterdam, stopping briefly at Freetown for extra coal bunkers on the way. Even the notorious Bay of Biscay was kind to us and the voyage was un-eventful. I was paid-off soon after arrival and returned to England and finally release from my Indentures.

As a result of this hi-jacking experience, I decided that after I passed my Second Mates Examination, I would seek employment with a "liner" company, whose ships were on fixed runs, and doing voyages of a more defined duration. I was confident that the choice of employment would be mine, because in 1953 most of the British shipping companies were still rebuilding their fleets and making good the losses suffered during the War. Consequently they were desperately short of qualified officers and jobs were easy to obtain.

(That is when I joined New Zealand Shipping Company trading to Australia and New Zealand. Their voyages of about six months seemed short and quite acceptable compared with the long voyages that were usual with Saint Line.)

34. Ashore for my 2nd Mates Certificate

It must have been about mid-April that I left the "Cape St. David " in Rotterdam. I know I spent my last weekend aboard watching the discharge of our cargo from Martadi in the Belgian Congo, into the long, Rheine barges fast alongside. These barges would then carry the iron ore to the industrial heartland of Europe. Typically the skipper's family were obviously living on board, and we could see his wife walking the baby in a pram up and down the deck. These families could have been Dutch, German, or Swiss and this had been their special way of life for generations.

This was the second time I had been forced to wait for the British consul to come back from a holiday and release me, but eventually I was signed off and on my way home, via the ferry from the Hook of Holland to Harwich and then home to Croydon in Surrey, with the prospect of being home for study over the next three or four months.

I can remember going to the Saint Line office soon after arriving home to sign the Release from my Indentures. I had waited over four years for this moment and I can still remember my non-committal answer to the question about returning to their employ when I had obtained my Certificate. In fact I had already resolved that when I was qualified, it would be with a Company trading to rather more westernised parts of the world and with voyages of shorter duration. No more 'tramping', with the possibility of being away from home for up to two years at a time.

It felt comfortable and warm being at home, but within a week I was bored. After spending four years at sea, my earlier school friends seemed distant and rather juvenile, and I missed the atmosphere of being with kindred spirits and the wonderful sense of freedom that a seafaring life creates.

Frankly, it never completely leaves you. I realised for the first time how one's environment can change a man and it took many years ashore to get used to the idea that one's behaviour was important as to how in the community viewed a person.

My mother was quite upset when I announced that to avoid the daily, lengthy and crowded commuter train ride to Navigation College in East London from Croydon, I had taken a room at the Merchant Navy Officers' Club in Wapping, known in the trade as the 'Stack of Bricks" Her response was "I suppose you'll only come home when you need your washing done." Mothers do not change, even though she was probably right.

35. The King Edward Seventh Navigation School

In those days, the College only catered for those studying for their 2nd Mates Certificates. Masters and First Mates studied, as I did later, at the Sir John Cass Institute in the City of London. This later spell of study was much more serious, because of marriage, and from the point of 'story telling', more conventional. During the period of study for my 2nd Mates Certificate I was determined to make up for those the stolen years of my apprenticeship spent at sea.

There was no age limit to qualify for an examination. The only requirement was that an individual had to have spent about four years aboard a ship — on Articles, as the saying went. This meant that those studying at the College were a mixture of ages and some had done their sea-time in the 'lower deck' and had not been Cadets but deck ratings. However, the majority of students were like myself and had served their time as indentured Cadets and were generally aged in their early twenties. Many originated from different places in the world, and particularly from the Commonwealth nations.

The plain fact was that all students attending the College were seamen and had that in common. This set them apart from perhaps a general college community. They may have served on ships owned by a wide range of Companies and been occupied in different Trades, but they somehow fitted into the same brotherhood and spoke the same language of the sea.

Naturally the subjects to be studied were all of a professional nature and connected with the world of the sea and ships. It is not always realised that a ship at sea is in itself like a town, and the officers running it must have the knowledge not only as sailors and navigators and all that implies, but to know how to cope with all the needs of a community, from medical, to electrical, to plumbing, to general maintenance, and have the knowledge and ability to deal with any emergency or situation thrown at them at any time.

The Examinations

The examinations themselves consisted of three parts over the course of a week. There was the written exam which was held over three days. This covered a range of subjects, including the mathematics involved in navigation such as trigonometry and spherical trigonometry, astronomy, actual navigation examples and chartwork, tidal calculations, radar plotting, ship stability and flotation, and

35. The King Edward Seventh Navigation School

engineering factors such as ship construction and stresses, electricity, etc, etc, etc.

The written examination would be followed by an oral examination, which could last for a couple of hours or even all day. This was in essence a test of nautical knowledge and covered a range that included the Rule of the Road, Light and Shapes to be shown, breaking strains of ropes and wires, the ability to splice or use bends and hitches, handling a lifeboat, and in fact just about everything the examiner could think of. The prospect of failure meant facing the dreaded penalty of being required to serve extra sea-time, usually three or six months, and served either 'on deck' or as an uncertificated officer aboard a coastal trader.

The third part of the exam was really the most straightforward, covering flag signals, the ability to send and receive signals in Morse Code by lamp, the signal flags, and various communications such as the verbal alphabet and radio procedures. In my days sending and receiving semaphore was included, but I believe this system is now part of history, though still used by the Navy

Before proceeding back to sea, the Company chosen would send us on a variety of professional study courses, such as Fire Fighting, Radar Plotting, Gyro Compass maintenance, etc.

The Gyro Compass course I attended was a hoot. There were three of us attending, and it was conducted by a retired Sales Manager of the manufacturer. We started at 9.30am and it was obvious that the whole exercise was really a PR job, and the greatest asset was going to the 'local' for a pub lunch, followed by a restful afternoon. The final day was Thursday, with a longer lunch, and but instead of a test to finish, we all snoozed at our desks, including the Instructor, before going home, each of us clutching a certificate to show we were competent enough to be put in charge of a gyro compass.

It was during this period that I learnt to fire a four inch gun, which was the typical armament of British merchant ships during wartime, or to shoot at drones, towed with very long lines by RAF planes with obviously very nervous pilots, using anti-aircraft Bofors guns fitted with gyro gun sights. Defence courses were part of our training — war was a constant threat in the fifties.

People I met at the College

One of the old sayings among sailors is that you do not have friends at sea, or what people ashore might call 'shipmates,' but such people were referred to loosely as "Board of Trade Acquaintances'. The same could be said of those we met at Navigation College. Friendships were shared, but in the main were of a temporary nature, with all of us knowing that once the exams, held every two weeks, were over, and each of us went back to sea, we were unlikely to catch up again, though in some cases our attendance for study at our next exams would coincide.

35. The King Edward Seventh Navigation School

Typical of this was membership of our college rugby team which was never a consistent Group. The exams were held every fortnight, and we would sit for them when we felt ready. Consequently, faces would come and go, and the Team would be constantly changing. The games for us tended to be taken quite light-heartedly, and viewed mainly as a means of having some fun and raising a thirst. Some oppositions questioned our conduct on or off the field.

Training nights were held regularly, usually consisting of a run to our favourite watering spot, The Prospect of Whitby in riverside Wapping, with thirsts added to by community singing, and then a three penny bus trip back to the College.

A few friendships were made and some people remain in my memory. One such was a fellow whose name was "Ginger" Stringer. Ginger was from Shell Tankers, and he was a racing car buff. His father owned a pub in Cambridge and this came in useful on many occasions.

Another I recall was "Spiv" Parker, so called because of his always immaculate appearance in the smartest of expensive suits.. His father was a Director of a large company and a source always of money. Spiv had an arrangement with his father's Saville Row tailor, whereby when Spiv needed funds, he would place an order with this tailor and by arrangement, the tailor would forward an inflated invoice, and give Spiv the balance.

I remember that we collectively agreed that the only item

of apparel that Spiv was lacking was a traditional Bowler hat — the symbol of a successful man in London. We won him one of these by bludging a ride from the Prospect one evening from a member of that City breed, and the prized hat was seen on the back shelf of the car. It left with us when we were dropped off in the West End a little later.

I was never really mechanically minded, but I would help Ginger prepare his racing car for the next Saturday's events and wear a white boiler suit, chalking up lap times on a blackboard. Tuning up times were famous for their copious lubrication with beer, usually followed by a trip into the City and a cheap feed of spaghetti in a little bistro which we regularly visited.

These antics came to an end when the car was written off in a collision with a lorry coming from the Covent Garden markets. I was buried beneath the offending vehicle, and woke up lying in the roadway with an unknown lady bending over me. I heard her say "He's so young" and I immediately passed out again, to wake up later in the fracture ward of the old Charing Cross Hospital.

This led to one of the most hilarious periods of my life. The fracture ward was located on the ground floor and my bed was next to the window. The Hospital itself was located in the heart of Soho's theatre land, and the street outside was always crowded. People would stop and sympathise with us; naturally we always pretended to be in agony, and they would pass in half full boxes of chocolates, or succumb

35. The King Edward Seventh Navigation School

to our pleas for some liquid refreshment, readily available from the Irish pub just across the road.

Being in a fracture ward, most of the patients were young like myself, and not seriously ill — most only hurt when they laughed — and were suffering from broken bones resulting from various sports or motor accidents.

In those days, many of the nurses in City hospitals were recruited from Ireland and were a cheerful and bonny bunch. Those working with young men in the fracture ward were mainly pretty, very relaxed, and enjoyed being relatively free of the tyrannical discipline then existing in the hierarchy of typical British hospitals at that time. They helped us keep our bottles of illicit drinks from the inquisitive gaze of the starchy Sisters, and often the night nurses would participate in our night time parties.

My injuries were actually quite severe at first and included a broken left shoulder and collar bone, and several left side ribs broken. The initial pain was bad enough, but worse was to happen. The ribs were strapped with heavy layers of sticking plaster around my chest. When the time came for the plaster to be removed, I remember the Sister, with a fiendish grin on her face, saying "Now is the time for my revenge — the joke is on you this time" She pulled the plaster off me in one swift move and spun me like a top.

There was a consolation. I remember a lovely honey-blonde physio coming to my bedside, saying it was time for "some heavy breathing trials". This was the very expression we used at the college when we had a date, but I still doubt if she really understood my look of anticipation.

However, there always seemed to be an affinity between nurses and sailors. Perhaps it was because both were subject to being more confined in their work or something. Many of my fellow seafarers married nurses, and often the first thing we would do on arrival at a seaport, was to contact the nurses' home, and arrange a party. These days, the nurses are not housed in 'homes' and therefore are not subjected to strict hours for themselves or their visitors.

A great prize finally came in the form of money. My father's solicitor arranged that I should sue the owner of the truck that hit us for damages and for so called 'pain and suffering'. If he had only known the fun we enjoyed in the hospital. Eventually, I received a cheque for the princely sum of 450.00 pounds. This was a fortune in those days, and a welcome subsidy for my time studying, especially when compared to the thirty shillings odd that I received every Thursday from my un-employment Benefit. It was some years later that shipping companies were forced to pay us Study Leave for up to three months.

Across the road from the College, was a well-known dockside pub called the Eastern Hotel. This was the final destination for the once pretty and then expensive West End 'ladies of the night', but we found out how kind and generous they really could be. We seafaring students were easily identified by our reefer jackets and it was obvious by Tuesday or

35. The King Edward Seventh Navigation School

Wednesday that funds were running low. These 'girls' would shout us a beer or two, knowing that we would repay them as soon we got our dole money on the Thursday. (This was the only transaction we would exchange with these ladies.)

I remember a fun night when we hired a stage side box at the local Empire Variety Theatre, known to sailors as the 'Sods Opera', and a landmark in those days near the Royal Group of Docks. This particular night starred an attractive lady who would dance in the nude except for a flock of pigeons that were trained to cover her most intimate parts. Naturally, we went armed with bags of bird seed, but try as we would, we were unable to coax the birds away. The outcome was that we ourselves were asked to leave.

This was the time of the current Queen's coronation, and a great time to be in London. One of the most popular guests was Queen Salotte from Tonga in the Pacific. I can remember her saying "I have British blood in my veins — my ancestors ate Captain Cook."

There were three of us, called the 'terrible triplets' at the college. We were very thick with nurses from the Westminster Hospital, and it was planned that on Coronation Eve, the six of us would have our normal boozy evening at the Prospect of Whitby, have our usual feed of spaghetti, and then armed with a variety of bottles, join the throng camping out in Whitehall for the night so we would have ringside seats for the passing parade the next day.

I remember being so cold in the greying dawn, especially

once the warming effects of the alcohol had worn off, but then being thrilled by the chanting of the young newspaper boys. There had been a series of nasty murders at that time in London and the bodies of two young women had been found the night before at Teddington. I can remember the cry of those newspapers boys to this day — "Another bloody murder — Everest conquered".

It was Edmund Hilary's and Sherpa Tensing's special Coronation present to the Queen, for after many years and many attempts by a variety of people, and causing some deaths, Mount Everest remained until then the Holy Grail of mountaineers. It had never been successfully climbed until that night.

The night we passed our Examinations

You will have gathered by now that at this time the pub 'Prospect of Whitby' ranked highly in our lives while sitting for our Second Mate's Tickets. They say that we should never go back and in this case it was certainly true. Many years later I was visiting London and out of pure nostalgia I decided to take a trip to Wapping. Not only had the whole area been transformed, but the old pub had suffered from "gentification". It just was not the same, though they had kept the old iron rings in the river wall, where in the old days the victims would be tied up, and it was left to the rising tide to drown them in the River Thames.

35. The King Edward Seventh Navigation School

In my day, the upstairs section was a classy restaurant, often frequented by the likes of Princess Margaret and people slumming from the West End, whereas downstairs in the noisy Public Bar the drinkers were entertained by three musicians playing guitar and ukuleles. If they were bribed with sufficient beer, they would play requests all night.

The audience normally consisted mainly of students from all over the Commonwealth, so the songs of the various countries, like Waltzing Matilda, and music from New Zealand and South Africa would be mixed with various baldy rugby ditties, such as "Now I am a bachelor", etc. There would be people slumming from the outside world, who could be easily coaxed into buying either the band or us 'regulars' sufficient quantities of refreshments to keep us singing. I can remember having many Birthdays regularly for instance during my three months at college.

In my day, the pillars holding up the ceiling were cut from old sailing ship spars, and coated originally with long gone varnish, but giving them a smooth surface. It was a long tradition that the piece of paper receipt we were given on passing our Certificates, as an interim mark of our success, would be 'dunked' in our beer (often repeatedly) and spread for all to see on one of these masts. I can remember about two weeks' after passing the exam, handing this horrible piece of screwed up paper to the Shipping Clerk in order to receive my proper Certificate, and his inevitable remarks about how well it had obviously been "dunked". It certainly had.

This night of celebration in question started in this traditional way, and then the three of us went into Town for a feed and more drinks. When sufficiently loaded, I can remember we 'purloined' some roadworks signs such as "No waiting this side" or "Go Slow" and intended to climb the fire escape at the Westminster Hospital nurses' home and fix these to our girl friends' beds. It was possibly a good thing that our progress to the hospital was interrupted by our being arrested by members of the Metropolitan Police, who were actually relieved to find we were quite harmless and very good natured though noisy and very drunk celebrating students.

Nevertheless, we were carted off to the famous Bow Street Police Station. I can remember our laughter when being charged, especially when the Sergeant said the bit about "Evidence being might be used against us" and my friend Ginger saying "They really do say that, Charley!"

Eventually, at about three in the morning we were told we should appear at the Court at eight o'clock that morning. I made the remark that our sleeping locations did not allow this time table and could they put us up for the night. The Sergeant grinned and said it would be a real pleasure. We were separated from one another, and with the clang of the cell door, my liberty was deprived; it just did not seem so funny after that.

35. The King Edward Seventh Navigation School

The next morning, after a cold sausage and equally cold cup of tea, our turn to come before the magistrate arrived, and he asked what we had to say for ourselves. I made the observation that it all seemed funny last night, but the joke was on us this morning. The reply I got was a classic — "That's the best speech I have ever heard in defence." The result was a Conditional Discharge meaning that no conviction was recorded, and we each had to make a contribution of seven shillings and sixpence towards the Court funds.

At that price, being locked up at the Police Station was really the cheapest night's lodging that was possible in London, even at that time.

Eventually all good things must come to an end, and it was time to get back to work, and to find another sea-going job. In those days it simply meant walking down Leadenhall Street where most of the British shipping companies were based, and deciding where in the world we wished to visit and how long we wished to be away on each voyage.

36. Leadenhall Street in the Fifties.

My only ambition from an early age, was to go to sea. This was an ambition stirred on by what was a part of our British heritage, the thought that each of us had a little salt water in our veins. Stories of Exploration, Drakes defeat of the Armada, Battles like Trafalgar, and the world wide gift of the Pax Britainia seemed to endorse the magic of just being British. I was still unashamedly British even as we saw the nation bankrupt and the crumbling of the Empire after WW2. I firmly believed in the lasting good that the British had given the world, even if the disputed colonialism and exploitation is disputed by a more socially conscious generation.

I was too young to serve during the war, I was only 13 when peace came to the world, but the memories of the time that Britain and its Commonwealth stood alone against the might and fury of Hitler's Germany were still fresh. I had been a youngster in London during the Battle of Britain and the Blitz, and then saw the Doodle Bugs and the V2 rockets.

I must confess that my greatest heroes were the men who had served in the Merchant Navy as civilians and who suffered the greatest casualty rate of any of the fighting services. The spirit that they displayed seemed still to be found within those of my generation that I was with at the Nautical College while studying for the 2nd Mates examinations. We were proud British sailors. It was 1953.

This spirit is spelt out in part of a Foreword to a book of seafarers memories, written by a man who was an Officer during this time — Sir Robin Knox-Johnston, CBE,.R.D,* and I quote in part:

"We were a lucky group, those of us who spent our early years in the British Merchant Navy in the 1950's and 60's. We were part of its last period of greatness, when the MN counted more than 4000 ships and 150,000 men We were trained by men who had gone to sea in "the Great Depression", been tempered by war, and were thoroughly professional. They did not see why we, as officer Cadets, should not be trained up to their exacting standards. We all felt part of being something special and were proud of the traditions we inherited."

The outcome of all this was that to a lot of us this sense of tradition, of responsibility and loyalty, to our mates and to our ships, came first and without question.

Although the time I write about was eight years after the War, British shipping companies were still rebuilding and making good the losses suffered during the conflict. Jobs therefore were plentiful, and young officers were greedily snatched up even as the ink on their new Tickets was still drying.

36. Leadenhall Street in the Fifties.

One street in the City of London was the local home for most of the most well-known shipping companies and was the target for people like me with a brand new 2nd Mate's qualification. It was Leadenhall Street, in the City of London. The street was perhaps a monument to years of so-called Free Trade, on which the wealth and influence of Britain was founded over the centuries.

Before starting the search for a job, the first question to ask oneself was "Where in this world do I want to go?" and the second was "How long do I want to be away?" though as a single person this second question was not so important, but I did not want to repeat my earlier mistake tramping trips of up to two years. I also rejected Oil Tanker companies because of their ships' short stays in port. (Rather like container ships today, so many years later)

With these questions in mind, one could start at one end of the street, concentrating on the main Companies, starting with Lever Brothers, the soap people who owned Palm Line, trading mainly to West Africa. (Hot) and then head West, to Furness Withy Line (North America and the cold North Atlantic) or to Royal Mail Lines to the West Indies and South America. (Nice ships and good run)

Then Elder Fyffe Line to West Indies for bananas (Tarantulas !) or the famous Cunard Line (cold North Atlantic again) or Union Castle Line, (passenger & fruit ships to South Africa) or to Clan Line (Australasia and Asia) or Prince Line (Mainly Asia) or Brocklebanks (India) Not to overlook the Ellerman Group (Everywhere) or then Elder Dempster Line (West Africa) or Ben Line (Asia) or Bibby Line (Asia) and British India Line (India) We should not forget P & O Line, with their fleets of passenger and cargo ships, and then the Houlder Brothers Line, to South America,

I am sure there were others, equally worthy of mention, but memory has grown dim over the years, and they, like so many others, have long gone out of business.

Because I liked Australia and NZ, I particularly considered Port Line, Shaw Saville Line, or New Zealand Shipping with Federal Line, all of whom had good ships and were well established companies, and they all had offices in Leadenhall Street. That trade, either via the Suez or Panama Canals, meant regular six monthly voyages, and this was very acceptable, when compared with Saint Line, with whom I had been apprenticed.

I selected and was accepted by NZS/ Federal Line, and never once regretted that decision.

I joined their relieving Dock Staff within two weeks, and was posted to my first ship, the M.V. Nottingham, a brand new ship known as the NZS Yacht, perhaps a month later, for a voyage to New Zealand, with general cargo outwards, and refrigerated fruit and dairy goods homeward.

After Thought.

I have often wondered how many fellow passengers on

36. Leadenhall Street in the Fifties.

trains destined to the main seaports of the U.K. would envy the lives of those confident young men sitting opposite them, if only it was known the destinations to which they were bound and that they were to be paid for the privilege of visiting. By contrast, for the ordinary person to visit such fascinating destinations would cost them thousands of pounds and for many, such travel would be out of the question.

The only clue to such a young man's purpose was perhaps the small wooden box he had with him. This contained his sextant, and was the personal 'badge' of the maritime navigator.

37. New Zealand Shipping Company

I have written about the thrill of traversing Leadenhall Street, then the home of so much of worldwide British shipping, after I had won my Second Mate's Certificate. The time had come to make a choice. I had decided that I liked Australia and New Zealand more than other places in the world, and the thought of regular six monthly voyages was a great improvement compared with those with Saint Line. I chose New Zealand Shipping Company, applied for a job, and was accepted.

It only took about a week for my appointment to be confirmed, and I was posted as Fourth Mate to their Dock Staff, the team that relieved sea going officers while they were on leave. My first ship was the famous 'Rangitata' in Albert Dock. Another officer also on 'Rangitata' who exceeded me by a few days in seniority was John Thorpe, who went on to become Master of the 'Bay' container ships, and stayed as a firm friend to the end of his career.

After a couple of weeks I was appointed as Fourth Mate to the 'Nottingham' which was known as the company's yacht because she was smaller than the average NZS refrigerated cargo ships, and was nearly brand new at that time. My best memory on joining her was the contrast between a modern ship and the older vessels of Saint Line. This was my first motor ship, and I remember being kept awake once we were at sea by the constant vibrations from diesel engines compared to the comparative silence of the triple expansion steam engine.

I still have fond memories of my first full Watch as we steamed down the English Channel. Quite apart from the pleasure of being in a modern wheelhouse surrounded by all sorts of gadgets, there was the intoxicating joy of that 'outward bound' feeling that never leaves a sailor, of freedom and escape from the rituals of the shore life, especially after a few months living ashore.

Life soon settled down into routine as we crossed the Atlantic. My first sight of the oil bunkering Port of Curacao, picturesque at night because of its fairyland of lights, yet horribly industrialised in daylight. Then onwards with the short voyage to the Panama Canal. It was my first view of that masterpiece of engineering, and lived up to my expectations. In those days it was completely dominated by the USA., and is only place in the world where the Master relinquished his command of the ship to the Pilot.

This was my first experience of the Panama Canal, the most common highway from Europe to New Zealand. Alternatively, NZS ran between Europe and Australia via the Suez Canal, so both routes became familiar to me. The other

37. New Zealand Shipping Company

alternative service was the MANZ run between NZ and Canada, but one that I never experienced. This was the world of the 'W' ships, whose names inspired many nom-de-plumes, such as the 'WhyWorry' and the 'Wotawopper'.

This was actually my third visit to New Zealand, and endorsed my love for that country. Some considered it backward and old fashioned, but I found it a gentle place, peopled by gentle and generous people of both Maori and European races. People would stop and offer us visitors a lift to town, or bring their families to visit overseas ships at the weekends, particularly in the smaller ports.

On this particular voyage and after discharging our general cargo we loaded a cargo of apples at Nelson, a delightful small town located in the Sounds, and in the heart of the then orchard area, though now famous throughout the world for its white wines. Who has not heard of Sauvignon Blanc from the Marlborough Sounds.

Nelson was a seasonal apple port for this reason, and the Company people would come from Wellington whenever there was a loading. The highlight of the loading season was the 'Apple Growers' Ball', barely remembered because of the cider consumed on the two occasions that I enjoyed the event.

It was during such an occasion loading there with the "Gloucester" that a lady guest remarked on the small stature of the Captain by saying "What a little Captain," to which he replied "That's why they have given me only a little ship."

The Cadet Ship "Durham"

I only did one voyage on the Nottingham, and on return to the UK I was transferred to the "Durham" at Falmouth in Cornwall. She was then being fitted out to return to work as a Cadet ship, carrying about forty Cadets instead of a regular crew. At that stage the Company had but one such Cadet ship, the "Rakaia". Later the two cadet ships would be joined by a third, the "Otaio".

Between these ships the Company had well over a hundred Officers in training, and who would have foreseen in the fifties that within the next 30years the Company would cease to exist.

NZS had been trading to NZ from the mid 1800's and it was a known order from the old days that sailing vessels should only overtake passenger steamships at night, so that the passengers would not be upset by being on a slower ship.

The Cadet Ship "Durham"

Those were a wonderful six weeks spent at Falmouth. It was a lovely summer, and there was little for us officers to do. I was Fourth Mate, and the Third Mate and I would spend alternative days as Duty Officer. I had an uncle with an old sailing boat there, and I spent most of my days-off sailing. I fact I very nearly did not live to tell the story, because while sailing alone well offshore one afternoon I carelessly fell overboard, and the yacht sailed on. Fortunately, she rounded up and I was able to swim to her, but I had difficulty in heaving myself back aboard, even young and strong as I was then. A lesson hard learnt.

Among the activities whilst there was the anti-rat fumigation, and I have told elsewhere the terrible smell caused by decaying rats in the Smoke Room.

The whole purpose after this time in Falmouth was for the Durham to become a school for future Officers. We carried two Second Officers one of whom was designated as 'Schoolteacher'. There was a Seamanship Instructor, a physical fitness person, and of course a Doctor. The ship was run on Royal Navy lines, and two bugle boys were employed so that the daily routine of raising and lowering the flags, known as 'Colours', could be observed. Wearing of correct uniforms was strictly enforced, and cadets were inspected before being allowed ashore. The Officers all took part in the teaching and enforcing discipline. To a high degree this was unlike life on any normal merchant ship.

There were compensations. The after deck was wood sheathed and surrounded by high nets when at sea. This meant that regular ball sports and matches could be played. A portable swimming pool could be rigged. I had the ship's carpenter make a scrumming machine from spare dunnage timber.

I really enjoyed my life on the Durham. I undertook the training of the Rugby team, joined in the deck cricket matches, and all the various activities. It was such a change from any previous life aboard ships, and in port we would issue challenges to any sporting body existing. In fact there was not a school or rugby team in NZ that did not beat us. We even challenged the Fiji national team while discharging in Suva. We only played fifteen minutes each half and they managed a score of perhaps 70-5 in that time. Our try was scored by a cadet, Charles Turner, who became famous overnight.

After discharging in various ports, we loaded apples in Nelson, and that was my first, best forgotten, visit to the Farmers Ball. I learnt that I had been put to bed that night by the lady guests of the Chief Officer. We went from Nelson to finalise loading in Wellington.

When we returned to UK we loaded this time for Australia. It is worth remembering the Officers we had for that voyage, because they are all involved in what later became the Durham Association, an association formed by previous employees of NZS. It is now a worldwide group. with branches in London, Liverpool, Melbourne, Sydney, Brisbane, Auckland, and Wellington.

Under Captain "Convoy" Hocken, we had 'Beaver' Bevis as Chief Officer, Dick Hannah as Second, Des Jones as School Master, myself as Third, and John Needham as Fourth. The ship's doctor was Colonel Campbell, ex Indian Army.

I did two voyages aboard the "Durham" — this one to New Zealand and the second to Australia, when the incidents below occurred. Most of my few years with NZS were pretty routine, with voyages to either New Zealand or Australia. I had postings aboard 'Nottingham', 'Durham', 'Gloucester' and 'Papanui', and it was aboard the latter that the story about the Migrant Dog took place. These postings were at various times interrupted by periods on Dock Staff. There are however, several episodes that stand out in my memory, and these are as follows:-

1. The Performance at the Princess Theatre, Melbourne.

During a visit to Melbourne aboard the "Durham' the stage musical "Kismet" was being presented at the Princess Theatre. My friend, Dick Hannah (Second Officer) had a local girlfriend whose old schoolmate was the leading lady. He was given four complimentary tickets for the Royal Box and I was invited to make up the four.

We decided that we should 'make a night' of it. Evening

dress and mess kits were the order of the day. The Chief Steward, Mr. Chapman, entered into the spirit, and arranged finger food to be served for our small party aboard the ship before the show.

We arranged our entry to the show to be spectacular, and it was timed so that when the orchestra and audience were in place, the impact on everybody would be at a peak. The reaction to four elegant young people arriving into the Royal Box was supreme.

Alas, the impact turned to sighs of anguish. I had purchased a large box of chocolates for the ladies, and this had been placed on the parapet. While taking off the fur coat of my companion, this became dislodged, and fell with pin point accuracy into the orchestra pit below, with most of the contents landing with resounding booms on the bass drum

2. Leaving Adelaide at Christmas time.

We had virtually completed loading at Port Adelaide, and we were due to sail for London the next day. The Captain's wife, well connected socially in Adelaide, had arranged a dinner dance on board for the Cadets, and for this reason the bugle boys had been re-assigned duties as gangway watch.

At the same time a bunch of junior engineers had decided to hold their own thrash, and this proved to be a very drunken affair.

The ships surgeon, Colonel Campbell, had invited several

of us officers to dine ashore, but was obviously unaware of Adelaide's then antiquated licencing laws. As our host, he had ordered several bottles of excellent French wine, each variety chosen to be suitable for every course asked for. He was somewhat surprised to have all these bottles delivered to our table at the same time, with the instructions that all had to be consumed within some time limit. Nevertheless, it was a delightful dinner and we returned to the ship about 9.30pm.

We were berthed at Outer Harbour, recently rejuvenated, and among the new beautifications were several young pine trees. I was last at this area in the mid-1990's and these trees were big and mature, but at the time I am writing about they were little more than seedlings.

We arrived back to the ship to find chaos around the gangway. Apparently one of the engineers had decided that he would not spend the forthcoming Christmas without the customary tree, and had gone ashore, ripped one of these seedlings out of the ground and marched back to the ship in triumph. Unfortunately, just short of the gangway he tripped and, he complete with the tree, fell into the water between the ship and the wharf.

This was the scene that greeted us. There were the Fourth Mate, the gangway lad, the irate Wharfinger, and a Harbour Patrolman, all trying to save the life of this drunken engineer. Between us, a rope was lowered into the darkness and eventually a voice said, "All fast — heave away." and up came the tree alone! With great difficulty we afterwards pulled the young man to safety.

The outcome of all this was that the Wharfinger retrieved his tree, we sailed without a Christmas decoration, and it cost the engineer about fifty pounds, and a big dent in his pride. However, at the later Christmas celebration at sea, he was given a special award for "Devotion to Duty".

3. Arrival at London.

This is an account of our arrival at London, as told by a then cadet, Geoff Morris:

"We got into the English Channel in early January — horribly cold, wintry weather — and expected to be on the train home by 20 January or so. But bad news greeted us. There was a strike by the dock workers in the London docks and we would have to anchor off Southend Pier until it was settled (which turned out to be fifteen days). So near to home, and yet so far.

While at the anchorage we went on to anchor watches. It was freezing cold; the ship was covered with ice and snow and we did very little in the way of work. It was tedious and boring and very cold.

When a ship is at anchor and over a certain length, and it's foggy, the ship's bell in the bow must be rung regularly every couple of minutes and at the stern, a gong must be similarly beaten.

37. New Zealand Shipping Company

I was on anchor watch and on the bridge one dark foggy night. My watchmate, Tony Batt, was up forward. He'd been ringing the bell diligently all night. When the time for the next peal arrived, he started, but after just a few rings, there was muffled cry and a sound of something falling to the deck — the clapper had become dislodged and hit him right in the mouth, damaging a few teeth. Bad timing, when we were about to go on leave! "

My own main memory of this time at anchor is that to avoid wearing out the same chart by constantly using the chart by marking our anchor bearings over the two weeks we were at anchor, I made a copy on the back of an old chart. This became a masterpiece of watch-keeper's' humour because every person who came to the chartroom added a drawing,

Royal Albert Dock, London

cartoon, or poem, so by the time we moved to Albert Dock after two weeks the chart was full of wonderful artwork. (I grabbed it as a souvenir afterwards.) Evenings at anchor were made bearable by the discovery of warm 'mulled' wine.

The Durham Association

My association with the DA started much later after I had been working ashore for some years. One evening during a private function while I was CEO at the Polly Woodside, I was sitting in my office and noticed that three strangers had entered the property inappropriately after 8 pm. I rushed out to tell them that we were closed to the public. One of the three looked at me, and breathlessly said "Aren't you Charles Treleaven, once an officer on the 'Durham'." It turned out to be Glen Smith, who was previously a Cadet, but who was now an airline pilot with an American Airline, under charter during the Ansett pilot strike.

It was from him that I heard about the DA, and on my next trip to London a few months later I had a pub lunch with Dick Hannah and John Needham, both of whom were friends aboard the 'Durham' and it seemed then that time had stood still. During the next day I attended a General Meeting of the D.A. and was impressed with the number of people there.

When I returned to Melbourne I met with two former NZS people who were trying to create interest among ex NZS people living in Australia. We organized a lunch aboard 'Polly Woodside', and later the Australian Branch of the Durham Association was formed among all those who had been connected with the Company, ashore or afloat.

Unfortunately, we are a dying breed. The Company went out of business in the 1980's so gradually those that served with NZS are now a diminishing team and are gradually "Crossing the Bar."

Lest we forget.

38. Union Shipping Co. of New Zealand

My time with this famous NZ shipping company was limited to about three years, and was really was only for a period of personal re-adjustment, after my divorce and losing my first shore job because of severe import control.

This was my first experience aboard a non-British ship, and I found the contrast was extreme. No longer was I required to keep nights aboard as a Duty Officer, leaving the ship at night in the care of an elderly watchman. Strict discipline seemed to be re-placed by Union rules. The general attitude to seafaring was quite different, and much down-graded. The compensation was that the pay was higher.

My first ship with the Company was the smaller of the Cook Strait ferries, the "Tamahine." She was on the daylight run from Wellington to Picton during the winter months, and relieved by the larger "Rangatira" during the busier summer months. This was an additional service to the two larger ferries that ran at night between Wellington and Lyttelton, in the South Island. All these ferries were replaced by the rail ferries in subsequent years.

The 'Tamahine' was infamous because it was said she would roll heavily 'on wet grass" and I found that at the height of a Cook Strait gale it was only with great difficulty that compass bearings could be taken, because of the list caused by the wind. The ships was not fitted with either radar or a gyro compass.

The trip across Cook Strait was known for its strong winds, and once we had cleared Cape Palliser we would often feel the full force of the wind. The trip was at first quite unnerving as a navigator. Often we would have as much a 25 degree allowance for leeway, and on the final approach to the South Island we seemed to be heading for the green hills. Quite suddenly a way through the land would open up and we would enter the narrow Tory Channel, leading us into the calm waters of Queen Charlotte Sounds.

4. Inter-Island Ferry, MV Tamahini

38. Union Shipping Co. of New Zealand

Such was the reputation of Cook Strait that many nervous passengers would turn green before leaving Wellington Harbour, even on a calm, fine day.

I have always said that the months spent as Second Mate on this ship were the best job that I ever had at sea. I had good friends in Wellington, and my girlfriend in Auckland would fly down and spend weekends with me. We spent every weekend from seven o'clock Saturday morning until two o'clock on Monday afternoon tied up in Wellington. What a job.

Apart from normal seagoing duties between Wellington and Picton, all we had to do was to supervise the loading of motor cars and other cargo. Must of the cars would be stowed down below, but a few would be lashed on deck.

I remember one terrible occasion that I was approached by the owner of a very fastidiously kept antique motor car who asked me to ensure that his car would be loaded last, and be kept on deck to avoid the possibility of the immaculate body suffering a scratch by being loaded below decks.

I told this gentleman that if he parked his precious car in a particular place that was never other- wise used, it would be safe and I would personally ensure it would be loaded carefully. No sooner had he followed my instructions, than a truck backed right into his vehicle, causing irreparable damage and even tears. I could not believe it.

I was about six months in this position, but all good things have to come to an end, and I was transferred to the famous island passenger ship 'Tofua'. This again was to me an idyllic situation, and I learnt to love the Pacific Islanders and their way of life.

The run we did was a dream, sailing from Auckland to Suva (Fiji), Niue Island, Apia (Samoa) and then Nuku'alofa in Tonga, and then home to Auckland. We carried about 200 passengers who arrived and left variously, reflecting the connection between the Islands and New Zealand, for trade, education and tourism. Passengers were mainly residents from the islands.

I only spent about two trips on this ship, but the "Tofua", and her sister ship the "Matua", were both ships much loved throughout the South Pacific because of their many years of service until they were replaced by various airlines from both Australia and New Zealand. My last voyage with Union Steamship was as second mate aboard the freighter "Waiana". She was a typical Union freighter, of about 5000 tons, and one of many of the then huge fleet of similar ships.

I joined her in Auckland and we loaded in Napier, Wellington, and Bluff, before sailing across the Tasman to complete loading our cargo for the Pacific Islands in Melbourne and Sydney. Ports of call included the now familiar Suva or Lautoka in Fiji, Apia in Somoa, and finally Nukualofa in Tonga.

The ship was not fitted for refrigerated cargo, but it was usual to load green bananas in Tonga, and during the voyage from there to Auckland, the bananas would ripen and be ready for the fruit market after discharge.

Normally this would eventuate perfectly, but on one occasion we ran into a cyclone that became almost stationary and we spent nearly a week just hove-to in appallingly rough seas. The result of this delay was that when it came time to discharge the cargo in Auckland, the cargo was just a mess of black, over ripe bananas, only good for composting.

There was in fact a sequel to this story.

I have never been a supporter of the Union movement, being fiercely independent and preferring to fight my own battles. However, in New Zealand it was not possible to get employment unless one was a member of the Union

MV Waiana at Sydney.

— except it was called the Officers' Guild. It was pretty militant and collectively it was nicknamed the "Kremlin" by outsiders.

At the time of one voyage away in the South Pacific there was a dispute between the Company and the Guild starting with a request for new toasters and finally the Guild called all Deck Officers out on strike. All this happened while we were away, but it became quite prolonged.

I was in a quandary. I had never before been on strike, and hated the very idea of being told what to do, and in any case felt the action was unjustified over such a trivial matter.

As we approached Auckland the tension on board rose, and the arguments as to whether we would comply or not became louder. The closer we got to Auckland the worse the tension became.

Finally, and to everybody's relief, as we enter the Hauraki Gulf, the gateway to Auckland, we learnt that the matter had been resolved, and the strike was over. I therefore never had to make the decision between sticking to my guns and not having a job.

I left Union Steamship after this voyage and decided to try to settle again ashore. I loved New Zealand and enjoyed good friends there and so I worked in several jobs, and even tried to start a small agency business of my own.

For various reasons, none of these endeavours proved successful, and I once more found myself back as a seafarer, doing the job that I really seemed to be was born for. I hated working ashore and I ended up aboard the island trader and oceanographic survey vessel "Taranui".

I joined her only for two weeks but stayed with her as Chief Officer for more than two very happy and interesting years.

39. Oceanographic Ship "Taranui"

Life can be full of contrasts, and those who do not experience the full diurnal range of existence are very lucky.

From early childhood I wanted to be a sailor. I remember that even before my teen years I loved wet weather and the sound of wind. We had a wrecked greenhouse — the blitz had blasted all the glass, and I spent hours on dark nights, in wind and rain, standing on a top shelf, with my head sticking out of the roof, pretending I was in the crow's nest of a tall ship rounding Cape Horn. I read everything from the book "Swallows and Amazons" to poems by John Masefield. I even subscribed my pocket money to a magazine called "Sea Breezes" — all about ships.

Clearly all I wanted was a seafaring career. I have explained elsewhere why I decided on the down to earth life of the Merchant Navy as opposed to what we called the "Grey Funnel Line" — the Royal Navy like my brother. I went to sea as soon as I could at sixteen and served my cadetship with the Saint Line, changing to the New Zealand Shipping Company when I qualified to be an officer. This meant that I could be on more regular voyages, usually only six months at a time, from Britain to Australia or New Zealand. By our standards, these were short trips.

Eventually, I became disillusioned with my life at sea because I had fallen in love. During the spell ashore for one of my examinations, I had met a girl named Sally. On subsequent voyages I was tortured by the separation from her, and I was much relieved when my seatime allowed me to come ashore for my next examination and to spend some months at home, at Maritime College.

We were married — a partnership founded in heaven! I only made one more voyage after our marriage, and I knew I could not endure the separation from my wife any longer. At the end of that voyage aboard the Gloucester, I resigned from NZS, and we decided that we would build a life together in New Zealand.

The company I had my first shore-side job with was an importer of floor covering. I approached them with some trepidation because I had no experience ashore. My fears were compounded when the Director interviewing me threw his pencil down and pointed out that he had some of the best salesmen clamouring for the job and asked me why he should even talk to me. Behind him, he had a picture of a large yacht, which actually at the time was the best yacht in the Auckland Squadron..

My answer was straight forward. "I am willing to learn. I have always worked hard, and you would have a bloody

39. Oceanographic Ship "Taranui"

good navigator for that yacht." The pencil was picked up again, and I got the job, but in the end import control beat me and I was made redundant.

I remember well the cold wet afternoon that I was sitting alone in my home in Auckland, feeling sad and useless and completely down in the dumps. All my hopes and dreams were shattered. My marriage had broken-down and I had been declared redundant from my first job ashore because of severe import control recently imposed.

My only qualifications were in sea-going technology that I thought I had renounced.

My misery was disturbed by the telephone ringing. I nearly did not answer it initially — but I'm glad I did.

A strange voice said — "I believe you are an ex seafarer"

MV Taranui

and when I agreed, it went on — "I have a small ship under charter to the NZ Government doing Oceanographic Survey, and I need a Second Mate for two weeks. Would you be available?" I could barely hide my excitement when I said that I could just fit that in.

"If I send you round an air ticket, could you fly down to Wellington on Friday and be ready to sail the next day?" It was just as simple as that, and at least it meant that I would eat for the next two weeks.

Little did I realise that this was but an overture to one of the happiest and most interesting periods of my life. I can still re-live that afternoon we sailed from Wellington and recall that special 'outward bound' feeling known only to sailors. I joined the ship as Second Mate but after that first voyage, I replaced the owner as Chief Officer, and stayed for more than two years.

The memory of my first view of the Taranui is still in my mind. The taxi from the airport dropped me off at the waterfront, and as I walked around the corner of the dockside shed, I saw the ship for the first time. I nearly laughed out loud. Most of my previous ships had been the fine vessels of New Zealand Shipping, big and modern and built for the UK to NZ Trade. Here was a small vessel of under 1000 tons, and really not all that modern. She looked more like a tug than a trader.

When I joined her, the ship was about 35 years old. She had been built for the Queensland coastal trade, with accommodation for ten passengers, and in those days was named the "Bingara". In 1940 she was requisitioned by the Navy as a school ship to train sailors in anti-submarine techniques, and became the HMAS Bingara. Over the next five years she must have trained hundreds of RAN personnel.

After the war, she was sold to Nobel's, the Swedish dynamite company, and spent the next years taking explosives from Melbourne to New Zealand, and bringing cargoes of NZ soft woods back for the post war building explosion in Australia.

Now she was privately owned by a New Zealander, Captain Uhr, who all the time he was at sea had promised himself that one day he would be a ship owner. The post war period gave him the opportunity. Starting with a redundant Tank Landing Craft, picked up for a song in the Pacific Islands, he made a small fortune by collecting and selling the thousands of 44 gallon fuel drums left behind by the Americans after the hostilities were over in the Pacific.

Because the Taranui was built with passenger accommodation, she was perfect for the oceanographic charter offered by the NZ government and for carrying the various scientific groups needed by the different studies undertaken. These studies were so varied — from the study of sea-worms; to looking for hidden offshore minerals; to very deep water search for animal life, and even to conducting drift card tidal studies for new sewerage projects.

At this time we were working for the DSIRO, Dominion Science and Industrial Research Organisation, based in Wellington. The work we did was actually the first steps that New Zealand achieved in the field of oceanography.

No matter what the task, the ship was a cargo vessel and fitted out for handling general cargo. Therefore, the special equipment put aboard for each study group sometimes required a large measure of versatility and initiative, and could be a special challenge for the Chief Officer.

The ship was actually registered in Vila in the then New Hebrides, but our home port was actually Suva in Fiji. Our mode of operation was to spend four months doing the oceanographic survey work on the New Zealand coasts, and then trade for four months around the South Pacific, and then back to the NZ charter in an ongoing cycle.

The ship only had two Europeans working aboard, myself and Captain Matherson, a lovely elderly man. The rest of the officers and crew were Fijian, and a more wonderful bunch would be hard to find. The great thing about the Islands' attitude to democracy was that we were all treated as equal but never once was my authority questioned nor did I have any trouble with familiarity.

The ship was just small enough to fit on the slipway in Suva, so we did all our maintenance work there. I came to know Suva, and the surrounding villages that were home to our crew quite well, and the relationship was reciprocal. To this day, I have only fond memories of Fiji and its people.

Fiji and the Fijian Crew. The Taranui was the only foreign going Fijian ship at that time, and as the Chief Officer I was well known about town. I was called 'Mr Chief' or 'Charlesi' and I would often pause at a house on my way back to the ship after a visit to the night spot known as the Bulla Talli (The Good Life) Club and join in the singing.

The group would sit on mats around the kava bowl, slapping thighs and calling "Bulla" before drinking the evil 'washing up water tasting stuff', with children peeping out from behind curtains. I even entertained the local people with English songs I had learnt in the Air Raid Shelters during the war. I love singing, and shared this pleasure with the Islanders. They good naturedly put up with my intrusions. I was young, energetic, and laughed a lot so I guess we had that in common.

In the course of the time spent on general Trade we found the same friendship and hospitality around all the Islands. Fiji in those days was something of a Trade school centre for various trades and occupations, and those qualified could find good jobs everywhere around the Pacific. It seemed that wherever we went, some member of the crew would have a cousin or friend, and a party would be soon organised, always with ukuleles and singing.

The crew had a healthy disregard for all types of safety regulations, and I was kept on my toes with regard to things like Safe Working Loads and breaking strains of lifting gear. This was in the days before Health and Safety Regulations, and this crew would have caused many of today's Inspectors to have nervous breakdowns if the same Rules applied in those days.

The Fijian man is by nature a gentle person, but physically big and powerful. I can remember watching with amazement (and horror) when six of them 'topped' a derrick by hand, a job normally requiring an electric winch.

I also remember a time when the Bosun grabbed a New Zealand wharfie delegate by the scruff of his neck and held him over the ship's side, saying "One more word from you, my man, and I'll drop you in the water" I had to spend some time entertaining the union man after this to avoid a general waterfront strike.

There was also an occasion in Bluff, where a few of the crew were having a quiet beer, and trying to ignore the racist taunts of some very drunk local fishermen. I had to warn these alcohol laden idiots that if they did not shut up, these big Fijians would 'eat' them. Fortunately good sense prevailed and they never discovered how true my words would have been.

One of the things I loved most about the Fijians was a shared love of singing. To listen to them, with the Islanders love of harmony was really awesome. The Captain and I would sit out on the boat deck during a warm, lovely tropical night, and listen to the 'boys' singing. It was magic. My greatest memory from these occasions was to hear them sing the hymn 'There is a green hill far away' in their native tongue.

39. Oceanographic Ship "Taranui"

While on the New Zealand coast, we would use many of the smaller outports as a base for our scientific work, and we would offer the local Plunket Society the means to raise some money for their child minding service by holding a night of Island music. The sailors always stole the show. I also remember a couple of occasions where the local Maoris would join in.

Under the title "A Song to remember" I have written elsewhere how I grew to love the Fijian farewell song "Isa Lei" and I actually called my first yacht 'Isa Lei', and I remember my indignation when other boats would call us "Easily."

I remember particularly several events during our survey work. Whenever we were on a survey station we would use a mechanical grab for samples of the sea bed, then we would take a core sample, and finally we would also use an underwater camera triggered by a counterweight hitting the seabed. This camera would also be triggered when it landed on deck, and the Fijian sailors would delight in lying down alongside it to be photographed.

Another thing we did was to catch albatrosses with a fishing line, ring them for identification, and let them go. It was our practice for the scientists to cram into my cabin for drinks before dinner. I remember the occasion when in the middle of such a session we were interrupted by a huge Fijian at the door with an equally big albatross in his arms. This bird was huge and had a wing span of perhaps ten feet. The bird was wiggling in his grip when the sailor let it slip through his fingers and loose among us. Chaos is hardly a description of what followed.

Then there was the experiment of the Deep Water Trawl. This was aimed at finding out what creatures existed in the depths of the Pacific Ocean. The trawl had a net about 100 meters long, with a four inch mesh at the entry, tapering down to a fine net at the 'cod' end. To keep the net open, there was a steel 'diving plane' weighing about one ton, to which was attached the towing cable.

The whole contraption was aimed at working at up to 4000 meters depth, which meant that we had to have a huge drum to handle this length of wire, and a small motor to wind it up. This was on the fore deck.

The ship was not built to handle all this, and the only way we could stream and tow the net was from forward, using the anchor windlass as the main strong point, and with the ship going astern for a long period, even after taking most of 24 hours to reach the required depth.

Recovering the net was too much weight for the windlass alone. Its power had to be backed up by cargo winches, and finally the wire would be led to its drum via a snatch block on the Bridge front bulkhead. Even so, the weight of 4000 meters of wire plus the net was such that only when the ship dipped down in the ocean swell, that a few fathoms of the towing wire would be gained. It actually took over three days to retrieve the net.

I can remember the collective tension when the net was

sighted. We had thoughts of catching a giant squid or similar creatures of unknown size or strength and all of us were apprehensive. In actual fact, after three trawls, and over three weeks of exhaustive work, we caught only small fish with the most notable being Lantern Fish. These were small, with a long 'nose' that included a small phosphorous light that would attract prey in the dark depths.

This oceanographic work was very varied and interesting. From landing geologists on barren rocky islands, to simply filling drums with seawater to calculate the turbulence of the oceans, to cruising off New Plymouth and using drift cards to test the likely final destination from a new sewerage system. It was during this latter voyage that we discovered, thanks to the echo sounder, a sea mount that rose to about 30 fathoms below the surface of the Tasman Sea. It was a craggy sister to the famous Mount Egmont, and we named it "Mount Taranui", although later its position was further confirmed and professional oceanographers named it something else. After several attempts and the loss of one grab, we never retrieved a sample from its craggy nature.

In my memoirs I have written a section called "A song to remember." and included is the story of when the crew farewelled me with that beautiful Fijian song "Isa Lei". Suffice here is to say that I was emotionally overcome, leaving this ship and her crew in Raglan, NZ.

I have also added a story called "Magic Letter" and both these stories follow.

The happy memories of my two years with the ship "Taranui" will stay with me forever.

40. With a Song in my Heart

I will never forget the first time I heard the song "Isa Lei"
It was Christmas Day. The ship had just finished a refit in Suva and we had signed on a new crew. We were originally scheduled to sail that Christmas morning for Wellington to resume our scientific work, but I managed to persuade the Captain that the crew would appreciate a Christmas Day with their families, and so we put the departure back until 10pm. We had some time up our sleeve so a few hours were not critical. The Captain and I joined other friends for a traditional Christmas lunch at the Hotel Suva, and we returned to the ship in time for a short kip before we sailed.

It should be remembered that the Taranui was at that time the only foreign-going Fijian ship, and held a very special place in the sea loving hearts of the locals, and not just the families of crew — so when we went to mooring stations to leave harbour, the wharf was crowded with well-wishers as well as our crew making their last farewells — one gets rather used to saying goodbye when you are a sailor.

It was a beautiful, warm tropical moonlit night, fanned

by a gentle trade wind. The bright stars were reflected in the water, and the Southern Cross beckoned us southward. Imagine all this, together with the sound of the ocean surf breaking on the protective reef. It was a perfect scene.

I was at my usual station in the bow, on the foc'scle head, with the carpenter and a few sailors. The pilot was on board, and we were "singled up" ready to go. Eventually the order came — "Let go forward". The engines erupted into life, and slowly the ship moved stern first from her berth and then rounded up for the harbour entrance.

As we did, hundreds of voices broke into "Isa Lei", the Fijian farewell song. It has to be one of the most beautiful songs in the world. If you have ever heard an Island choir with their natural harmony, and the deep, deep voices of the basses underscoring the melody, you will not be surprised when I say that in this situation I was quite overcome and fighting back the tears. It was a special and magical moment, and in that idyllic setting too. A Hollywood scriptwriter, or even one of those old Fitzgerald travel movies, could not have set the scene better.

As we sailed into the night, lifting gently to the Pacific swell, I could hear those voices gradually receding, to become a memory that has never left me.

The Second Time I heard that Song
Lying between the two main islands of New Zealand is a stormy passage of water called Cook Strait. In those days, a

night ferry connected the North and South Islands, leaving Wellington for Lyttelton. A shorter daylight voyage, was another ferry route, from Wellington to Picton, now used by the rail ferries that have superseded all previous ferry services of the sixties. Incidentally, for a while I was second mate on the Picton Ferry, the Tamahine.

It was an attractive voyage to Picton. The ship would leave the shelter of the North Island, and would often crash her way against the westerly gales of Cook Strait. Sailors said that the Tamahine would roll on wet grass! As we approached the South Island, a small opening would appear in the headlands. This was Tory Channel, a narrow northerly entrance to the Queen Charlotte Sounds — peaceful inland waters, with scenic surroundings. That area now is the source of popular white wines

In 1963 the Queen and the Duke of Edinburgh aboard the Royal Yacht Britannia made a tour of New Zealand. The Royal Yacht, "Britannia" had sailed into Picton to carry them back to Wellington. The Taranui, as part of our oceanographic charter, had been surveying at the top end of the Sound that day. We were sailing back to Ship Cove, originally named by Captain Cook as a place of refuge, and used by us as an expedition base overnight — the scientists were strictly 9 to 5 people!

I was on the bridge, yarning with the captain, and looking astern I saw the shape of a New Zealand frigate, and behind that the unmistakable shining blue hull of the Royal Yacht.

I summoned the Bosun to the bridge. "Get all the hands you can to line up on the Port side of the foredeck" He acknowledged, and as he left the bridge I called after him "and be ready to sing!" I took the wheel, meaning there would be one more hand on the foredeck, and we rang "half ahead" on the engines. This was to slow down and to let the Yacht catch us quickly. We need not have bothered really. Taranui was flat out at about eleven knots, where as I could see that Britannia and her escorts were doing at least fifteen knots.

That convoy was going to overtake us on our port side. We planned that we would gradually edge up to port, so that the Royal Party would pass as close to us as safely possible. Now the VHF radio started blaring "Taranui — keep clear" We edged closer! So it went on, and the escort commander was obviously agitated — we could hear his concern on the radio.

The time came — and Britannia was alongside. As she came past, we could see the Queen and the Duke photographing our little ship. They were obviously surprised to see our ship registered in the New Hebrides, cruising in New Zealand's inland waters. But that was not all however; as the ships drew level, the Fijian crew started singing 'Isa Lei', and that beautiful song echoed between the ships. The Royals waved as they passed by, and our boys finished their song with three rousing cheers. It was again, a memory to cherish, forever.

The Grand Finale — The Third Time.

I went for two weeks, and stayed over two years as Chief Officer aboard Taranui. I think that those two years provided me with some of my most cherished memories. It was a period in which I reconstructed my life, a period of regaining confidence, and period of professional involvement. In pursuing the oceanographic survey work and handling all sorts of specialized equipment with only the gear available on an ordinary cargo ship was constantly challenging. If you look at ships built specifically for that job with all their fancy gear, you will understand what I mean.

Even during the times we spent back in the Islands were memorable, but especially I remember the fun and hospitality of the Islanders themselves. This was enhanced because everywhere we went, even those small remote atolls, some of the crew would have relatives who would open up their homes and hold a welcome to us all. I was single and young enough to join in, and although we were trained to normally maintain a certain distance between ourselves and the "lower deck," the Island approach to democracy was relaxed, and never once did I have trouble with crew taking advantage of friendship.

The way we came off charter in New Zealand, was to travel "light ship" — without cargo to Melbourne. There we would load for Suva, mainly flour and bully beef, known as Bullamacow in Fiji, together with the odd motor vehicle. I had always to allocate some space in the holds and on the poop, for the old sewing machines and pre-loved furniture that the crew would buy for their villages in Fiji. The Islanders had no sense of possession, everybody owned everything.

I have written elsewhere about those fabulous two years aboard Taranui, both around the Islands and in New Zealand waters with the scientists. Suffice to say, a special rapport built up between myself, Captain Matherson, and the Fijian crew.

Sitting out on the boat deck in mid-Pacific on a Sunday evening, with the crew singing hymns in those marvellous Fijian voices was atmospheric. It was a bonding experience for all of us working and sailing together in a small ship. We were doing things together, such as running a ship's concert party to raise funds for small town Plunkett Societies throughout NZ, and sharing both fair and terrible weather.

I realized however this life could not go on forever. I would need to regain a more established and less idyllic existence.

At a previous visit to Melbourne I had secured a job as a deck officer with the British Phosphate Commission on Melbourne based ships that ran to Nauru and Ocean Island for phosphate. The owner of Taranui therefore arranged for me to be relieved in Raglan, a small seaport near Hamilton on the west coast of the North Island.

The day arrived to leave the ship. With mixed feelings

40. With a Song in my Heart

and with a heavy heart I stowed my gear for travel to Melbourne, showed my relief around the ship, and had a final wee dram with Captain Matherson — by now a dear friend — and prepared to leave.

A small tug came out to the anchorage to take me ashore, and the Bosun organized all my gear to be loaded aboard.

The crew assembled on our foredeck and after lengthy farewells I finally stepped aboard the tug. Unknown to me, a young journalist from the Hamilton newspaper was aboard the tug and was a witness to all this emotional farewell. After 40 odd years, I am sure that this no-longer-young man will not object to me using his words. My modesty precludes my own efforts, and in any case he says it better than I ever could.:-

"As the officer, Charles Treleaven, shouldered his pack and stepped from the Taranui for the last time, the crew lined the rails. There were no awkward speeches or tearful farewells, but at a sign from the bosun — Billy Baleilikusavu — they began to sing in their native tongue. As the tug pulled away the crew said their last farewells with the haunting strains of their traditional parting song — "Isa Lei". As the gap widened between the ship and the tug, Charles stood at the stern and saluted the singers. In a voice that was not quite steady he called "Thank you, God bless you all, and Goodbye."

Now you can see why that song means so much to me — so many magic memories and so many magic moments.

When all else fades, and whatever Fate brings, I will still have that song "Isa lei" to remember. It is truly a Song in my Heart.

41. The Magic Letter

It all happened during my time as Chief Officer of the 'Taranui', and started when we were berthed in Suva, Fiji, having just returned from New Zealand and the Oceanographic Survey work we did there. Our annual survey was due, needing attention to hull and cargo gear maintenance, crew change, and a host of other things designed to make a Chief Officer earn his salary.

This all required piles of paper work, and I was struggling at my desk to cope with it. My cabin opened on to a cross alleyway, and I had my door open because of the heat — no such thing as air conditioning in those days.

There was a gentle tap on the door. I looked up and there was a small, skinny kid, about eight old years and of obvious Indian extraction. I quickly looked around to make sure there was nothing of value lying around — one gets a bit cynical in the real world.

"Can I do anything for you, Mr. Chief?" he asked.

"You can leave me in peace "I replied. "Go away" Over years at sea, often the only foreign language we learnt was how to get rid of beggars — "Impshi Allah "(Go to

Hell) to emphasize my wish to be left alone.

"Mr Chief, please let me do something for you. My father is dead and I have to look after my sick mother and my little sister"

"I suppose your dog died yesterday" I resorted to hackneyed responses.

"No" he replied earnestly "We can't afford a dog. But please let me do something for you"

There was something appealing, something special with this lad, so I relented. "Can you polish shoes?" "Yes Mr. Chief" he said. I took a couple of shore going shoes out of my locker and some cleaning stuff.

"You take one shoe at a time outside my cabin, where I can see you, and bring that back, then take the other"

He set to work with a vigor only seen with the shoe shine boys in New York. What a job he did — I was going to look like a Guardsman in my next spin ashore. When he finished I gave him a little loose change — it wasn't much but he was obviously surprised and grateful.

It was time for lunch and the gong sounded in the saloon. "Are you hungry, lad?" A silly question really, because he was only skin and bones "Come with me, then." I walked him to the galley to meet our overweight Fijian cook. "Can you find something for my little friend to eat?" I asked. "Yes Boss" — so I left them to it.

I learnt later that not only had my little friend eaten himself to a standstill, but he had scrounged enough for

41. The Magic Letter

his family as well — probably enough for a week by their standards.

Anyway, I was left in peace and that was the main thing.

The next day, I returned to my cabin after inspecting the bilges, to find him standing by my door. He had by now persuaded the whole crew that he was my lifelong friend, and he had the run of the ship.

"Can I do anything for you today, Mr. Chief." I thought about it. "Yes, these letters need posting, do you know how to do that?" He assured me that he had been posting letters all his life. These were already stamped, so no money was involved — But I was wise enough to let him know he would be rewarded on his return. Strangely, he returned at meal time, received a little reward from me, and headed off to his special friend — the cook.

The next day — the usual question "Can I do anything for you, Mr. Chief."

I then decided to really test him out. I gave him a shopping list of small items like toothpaste, shoelaces, a comb, and similar things, plus some money. Certainly not a fortune, but even so I would not have been surprised if I never saw him again.

A little while later he returned, handed me the goods, and some small change.

In this way, he endeared himself to me. Every day I found something for him to do, or some shopping, usually fruit from the market which we would share. He ate with the cook, and dutifully returned home each afternoon, I suppose, to his family with the day's loot.

We were in port for about a fortnight, and then our departure day was looming. We were heading back to New Zealand and would not return for something like four months. The young fellow was distressed.

"What will I do? How will I feed my family?"

I pondered on this for a while, and then on my little portable typewriter I wrote a letter of reference on the ship's stationery, and signed it with a flourish

"Here" I said, "Here's a letter that says what a good lad you are, how honest you are, and how helpful you can be. That's the best I can do for you. Show it to people who look rich and see what happens." I also handed him some clothes that I had bought for him.

We sailed for New Zealand that afternoon, returning to Wellington to resume our scientific cruises. It was a busy time and I had hardly a moment to think about anything but work.

When you are busy, time passes quite quickly, and soon we were bound again for Melbourne to load the usual cargo for Suva and to return to our Island trading. Suva had become like a second home to me, and I realized that I was either stateless, or a real citizen of the dying empire. An Englishman, nominally living in New Zealand, working on a Fijian ship, and calling Suva my home. It was so

41. The Magic Letter

confusing that I did not know to whom I should pay tax — I never sorted that one out!

So approaching Suva was like coming home, and as we tied up at the wharf after perhaps three months away, guess who was waiting with big smiles and looking very smart in new clothes? As soon as we rigged the gangway he was first aboard and came rushing up to me.

"Mr Chief- Mr Chief" he was so excited he choked on the words. "That was really a Magic Letter"

He explained. In those days the big American cruise ships of the Matson Line would visit Suva and land parties of tourists to look around. Apparently my young friend would identify a group of elderly ladies, probably rich and widowed, and offer to show them Suva and its leading features. He would show them the letter, to establish his credentials in that way. On return to the ship, they would tip him, not the few coins he would previously have begged for, but $10 or $20 notes. He had become rich beyond all bounds.

This was my last time in Suva and the end of another chapter in my life. I would eventually leave the Taranui in Raglan, New Zealand, and fly from Auckland to Melbourne and join the beautiful "Tri-Ellis" of the British Phosphate Commission.

I have often thought about that young fellow. I am sure he has had a successful life because if anyone was going to pull himself out of poverty, it would be this boy.

But as I write these happy memories, I can still hear him

calling "Mr Chief- Mr Chief" and I now realize one thing. I never even knew his name.

42. The British Phosphate Commission

When I served aboard the "Taranui", we would come to Melbourne on the completion of each four month period of oceanography. This was to load staples of the Fijian diet, bags of flour and cases of tinned corned beef, for Suva. I remember the corned beef was known in Fiji as "bulla-ma-cow."

While we were loading, many of the Fijian crew had relatives studying at Melbourne's colleges, and frequent parties for them were held aboard the ship, with much singing and laughter.

Although born in London, I had become used to the smaller sized buildings of New Zealand, and the sight of the tall structures of Melbourne was to me quite awesome. I also realised that I had been missing normal living, and although I enjoyed the free way of life of the South Pacific, I knew that sooner or later I would have to revert to a more suburban way of living.

During a visit to Melbourne, I made inquiries about a job with the British Phosphate Commission, which had ships running to Nauru, Ocean Island, and Christmas

Island, taking supplies to them, and bringing phosphate fertiliser back to Australia. It was subsequently arranged that I would leave the ship 'Taranui' in Raglan, the port for Hamilton, NZ. then fly to Melbourne to join the 'Tri-Ellis' there.

The Commission had four ships, but the two most modern, Tri-Aster and Tri-Ellis, were running to the Pacific islands with their home port as Melbourne. On the trips from Australia, we would take supplies of food and water and passengers to the Islands and bring phosphate back to either Melbourne or Geelong. At Nauru or Ocean Island we would load 12,000 tons in about ten hours, using special conveyors, whereas the discharge in Australia would take nearly two weeks.

The average voyage took about twenty days, but because the sea currents at the Equator could be strong, and the island moorings rather flimsy, we would face the occasional 'drift' as it was called.

During a 'drift', the ship, in common with other ships waiting to load, would sail up to the loading area, but if conditions were deemed to be unsuitable, we would simply drift to where ever the sea would take us, to try again next day. The longest drift I ever endured was over forty soul destroying days, each day without any sense of purpose or the usual feeling of going somewhere.

It was during a drift once over the Christmas period and we were celebrating New Year's Eve, that while I was having

42. The British Phosphate Commission

a quiet drink with the Captain and a couple of the other Officers in the Chart Room, we were interrupted by the Old Man's 'Tiger' as his steward was known. He was actually very drunk, and after repeatedly wishing us all the best things possible for the New Year, over and over again, he squinted at the barometer carefully, which he had mistaken for a clock, and then pronounced that it was time he went to bed.

I had seen the 'Tri-Ellis' in port previously, and had often remarked on her lovely design, particularly her spectacular clipper-ship bow. When later working aboard her, I found that this feature was designed because of her job, which was to periodically check the mooring anchor at Nauru which lay some 6000 feet deep at the edge of the coral reef, and the buoys. Under this shapely foc'sle head were installed the winches and capstan large enough to handle the 6000 feet of cable. (I can remember wishing we had had such equipment when using the deep-water trawl aboard the Taranui.)

MV Tri-Ellis leaving Auckland

Only once during the time I was aboard did we perform this tricky task, which required a high level of skill and seamanship. It took about three days, to lift the anchor from that depth, inspect the chain, and service the shackles.

Re-laying the anchor meant lowering the anchor to the prescribed depth, and then steaming slowly towards the Island, watching all the time the leading marks, until the anchor would ground at the right position. The cable would then be attached to the span wires running to very large buoys, whose buoyancy would keep the whole system in place by their tension.

It is worth noting that these moorings were destroyed during World War Two by the evacuating British, and during the five years of occupation, the Japanese failed to load even one ship load of phosphate simply because they were not able to organise the moorings.

The time we spent discharging in either Melbourne or Geelong gave time at home to any crew member who lived locally, and I learnt the great difference between British and Australian ships. At that time on even lowly British tramp ships, an officer was on duty with 'nights aboard' all the time, whereas on the Australian equivalent, the ship was virtually deserted, and left in the care of a Watchman who was usually a pensioner. It may be different these days.

Even the allocation of jobs was different then. My most important occupation on joining the Tri-Ellis was the calculation of every crew member's weekly wages, even including

42. The British Phosphate Commission

the Captain, and unless they had arranged for money to be sent to a relative or Bank, they had to be given cash each week, even at sea. I found that when overtime was included, the Captain was about number four on the payroll.

Because I had no home in Melbourne, a taxi driver took me to a motel in South Yarra, which I adopted as my home whenever we were in port. If the ship was berthed in Geelong, the Company would arrange a bus each day to bring the sailors to Melbourne and again take them to the ship each morning.

The motel I adopted as my home was known as the 'South Yarra Fornicatorium' and included was the 'Lair Mother', who was a middle aged ex-British Airways hostess, who boasted that at one stage she had been engaged to three different men in three different countries at the same time. Her name was Ruth and she would hold court with the younger residents in her room.

I got to know Ruth pretty well, and she took me under her wing. She reckoned that I was not meeting the right type girls, and consequently went out of her way to arrange dinner dates with young ladies that met her standards. One day, she said that there was a girl who worked at the US consulate, but that she did not warrant a dinner but only a lunch. Consequently, a lunch date was organised and I met Elaine. When I told Ruth that I had asked Elaine for further dates, she thought that was so stupid and wasteful.

Later, when Elaine and I were married, Ruth was a guest

at the reception. She became very drunk, and constantly called out "This will never work" At the time she was eventually escorted from the gathering. Time showed her to be right but it took about 14 years for her prophesy to come true. Sadly, Elaine and I became eventually divorced.

One of Elaine's friends had a husband, Peter, who became a very close friend to me. In fact, he was Best Man at our wedding, and for the Stag's Night before hand he brought along six of his buddies, knowing I knew nobody in Melbourne. It was through these connections that I got later involved with business and sailing. They all remained as close friends and only death has diminished their number.

I actually resigned from the Commission when I got married, intending to work ashore afterwards. The Master of the Tri-Ellis, Captain George Bridges, was a guest at the wedding. George was one of the tallest men I have ever met, and when asked how tall he was, he had a stock answer — "Seven foot six, with an umbrella up."

It was soon afterwards, that the people of Nauru won their independence from Britain and the Republic of Nauru was proclaimed, that the British Phosphate Commission itself was wound-up, and all their ships were sold.

This finally ended my career as a seafarer but I kept in touch with the sea by sailing and of course with my later job as CEO of the restored sailing ship Polly Woodside. My years as a ship's navigator also proved useful experience in the time that I taught astronomy to school pupils all over Victoria.

PART 3.
MY LIFE ASHORE.

43. Lumacell Plastics Pty. Ltd.

When I resigned from the Phosphate Commission, I finished my career as a seafarer. I married Elaine and decided to find work ashore in Melbourne, though I had no job and no shore profession. I knew I would have to start from scratch.

Through Elaine, I became friends with a young BHP executive who persuaded me that a job as Sales Representative with Shell Oil would be a rewarding career. I applied for a position, was accepted, but because the training course for Sales representatives was not due for some months, I was given a job in their travel advisory section.

This was really a hoot. Here was I, a pommy seafarer, ignorant of the hinterland of Australia, giving people travel advice on the best way to get to places I had never heard of. We had a library of travel information that was in great demand by the travelling public. My job was simply to satisfy their inquiry — "You tell me where it is, and I'll tell you the best way to get there !"

Needless to say, I did not last long in that job, and was shifted into the Contracts Division. This was a period where their old card system was being upgraded for a computer, so my job was to transfer information to a form ready for the I.T. Expert. I found this work very boring, and tedious, and vowed I would find other employment.

Using my short experience as a 'Sales Manager' in New Zealand, and a great deal of exaggeration, I became appointed as Assistant Sales Manager for a division of Australian Paper, then one of Australia's largest companies.

I was in charge of exploring the markets for their first entry into the world of plastics. They had just negotiated an arrangement with a South African company, based in Paarl, near Johannesburg, and who had pioneered a large market in fruit packaging with their expanded polystyrene apple trays. APM had a large market with papier- mache trays, but wanted to see if expanded polystyrene was a replacement material.

I initially explored this market in Australia, but as it was only intended as a research product and not to gain sales, I was told to keep clear of competing with their apple rays. This was pretty frustrating, so I concentrated on markets in other areas such as meat packaging, retail fruit marketing, catering products, and general packaging.

Of all these products, I found that a viable market existed in retail meat packaging, and tried a sample range of trays, to replace the currently used pulp meat trays, which tended to become soggy with blood. Actually, APM were not keen to enter this market either as the main manufacturer of

43. Lumacell Plastics Pty. Ltd.

pulp meat trays was also a good customer for their paper and cardboard.

In the course of this work, I also researched suitable laminated foam products for the catering area, and this brought me into contact with Mulford Plastics, a company which handled clear sheet plastic that was suitable for lamination. Their local Director was Alan Mee, who became a personal friend and who invited me to go sailing with him. This ended up as a regular Saturday event.

I can remember one stormy afternoon on the Bay, when he asked me if there was any future in foam polystyrene sheet (EPS). I can remember telling him that I wished I had something like $50,000 capital so I could start my own business and exploit this material's value.

It was a few days later that Alan called me and asked if I could take a trip to Sydney, as his Company were looking for local manufacturing diversification, and perhaps EPS foam sheet would fit their ambitions.

The outcome of all this was that at the subsequent Board Meeting, it was decided to proceed with the venture. A new Company was to be formed, to be called Lumacell Plastics Pty. Ltd. and I was to be awarded one third of the shares and to act as general manager of the company.

Another great moment was that at the commemoration dinner afterwards, the company drink was adopted. It was the Brandy Cruster, remembered to this day for its Lumacell connections.

Premises were found at Moorabbin, a local engineering company were commissioned to make the extruder, and a trip to Japan secured a simple vacuum forming machine. The cutting of the products from a multi-formed sheet was performed at a second operation with a modified cutting press.

I had persuaded an operator from APM to join me in the venture. Together we would make the sheet for three days, and then convert this sheet into products for the balance of the week. The cutting operation and packaging of the product was done by two local Italian girls. Sales were gained by me visiting main supermarkets and meat companies. We had a major celebration when in one week we packed 5,000 trays.

This small pilot manufacturing venture meant going to the factory on a Sunday evening, starting the extruder, and running it for 72 hours and taking it in turns to sleep on the office floor. I spent Thursday and Friday chasing up sales, while the other crew made the products.

I well remember that soon after we had installed the equipment, and appeared to have a business operation, we were inspected by the Chairman of Mulford Plastics, Sir William Kilpatrick of international fame. All was well set up for this auspicious occasion, but at the vital moment I managed to blow the head off the extruder.

From this small, rather backyard operation grew a major packaging company, employing over 120 people, producing over 6 million trays per week, and with Sales offices in every main State throughout the Commonwealth.

In those early days I was involved with sailing, and I can remember well the occasions I had to ring the skipper to make my apologies because I had to fix a machine. Then, as the business grew and my personal improved, others would say I was "lucky" in my position. There is no such thing as luck, only hard work and dedication.

We were guilty of initially filling the local rubbish tip with our offcuts because we were forced to use pre-gassed, imported materials, and could not use the off-cuts. However, developments in technology allowed us to replace this pre-gassed material with un-gassed raw material and pump in the Freon directly into our extruders. This meant we could re-process our own waste and using reclaimed material thus increased profitability and avoid polluting the neighbourhood.

Packaging plastics later in the 1970's came under pressure from those worried about their effect on nature and the environment in general. I remember a call from an executive of one of our large Groups saying that he has people tearing up packaging in in one of their shops.

We convened a meeting at the Plastics Institute to discuss this and I was elected as Chairman to defend the Industry. Our body was called 'Plastics and Solid Waste'. I can still remember the arguments we used to defend the Industry, some of which were blatantly loaded in our favour, but some of which are still valid today. I have not been involved for a long time and will not launch into this debate here.

Later, it was found that the Freon gases we employed in our extruders, though used elsewhere, mainly in refrigeration, were affecting the environment in changing the ozone layer, and their use was partially banned.

However, this was later, and after ten years and I had already become uninspired by little white trays and I sold my shares in the Company. Afterwards I spent some time as a consultant for the United Nations Development Program based in Amman, Jordan.

My life there-after turned a full circle, and I returned mainly to things maritime in the fascinating position of restoring the old coal hulk Rona, that I had first met in 1951, into the beautiful Polly Woodside. I spent eleven years as CEO on this wonderful task, and when I decided to leave I decided that I should use my experience as a seagoing navigator to teach school children basic astronomy. Life was indeed a full circle.

I was aged 61 when I started this venture, which I called 'Journeyman Education Services'. I found that the whole world of teaching and mixing with youngsters really excited me and was very satisfying. I said later, when I retired over twenty years later, that I really should have been a teacher all my life. Perhaps the rest of my life was preparing for this final career, and without those experiences I would have been floundering.

But that's another story. However, several things happened during these years, and these are told as follows.

44. The Citizens' Action Group

It was on a cold winter's Wednesday evening, with the whole of Australia locked-down by labour disputes and strikes, mainly caused by the rampant inflation.

The strikes affected everybody. Shops could not get deliveries of essential supplies, fuel for our cars was restricted, but worse still, our defence forces were hampered. The Navy could not go to sea, and the RAAF were grounded by lack of fuel.

I can remember reading that evening's Herald newspaper. (We used to get an evening Herald in those days) and a particular article with a headline "Australia is going to the Dogs, and nobody cares." I can remember hitting the coffee table in front of me and saying "Well. l I bloody well care"

The next morning I telephoned the Herald, to be told that the journalist who wrote the article was not employed on a permanent basis, but would I like to speak to somebody about this. Eventually I was put through, and then asked who I was and who did I represent. I had to do some pretty quick thinking and replied "The Citizens' Action Group". Corny as it was, the name stuck, and then the journalist asked a few questions about what we stood for and our general beliefs. Afterwards, I did not know what an outcome would happen. It was like an avalanche.

This all was published on the Friday evening, and although I gave no name and phone number, I was tracked down by many people with the same views. By Sunday afternoon, I had many pages of an exercise book filled with names and addresses, and I was a bit overwhelmed, wondering what to do next.

I had no political contacts — I was a simple sailor and still virtually a stranger in Melbourne. Then I remembered that the Chairman of the company that backed my plastics business had at one stage employed Don Chipp as a salesman after they had both left the RAAF in 1945. With this rather loose contact I rang Don Chip that evening at home. He was at that time Shadow Minister of Customs in the Liberal Party, under Billy Sneddon, the leader of the Opposition.

I was surprised by Don's warm and friendly manner, and he invited me to meet his colleagues next day at the Federal offices in Flinders Street. I can't remember all the names, but here was hierarchy of the Liberal Party who welcomed me as an-anti Union person. I realised that I was in danger of being used as a puppet for political purposes.

One of the very objectives in the CAG 'manifesto' was for the Action Group to build a bridge across the political divide, and I realised that I needed to talk to the other Parties. From that meeting I went to the main office of the Labor Party,

44. The Citizens' Action Group

and met with their Secretary. I could see that he treated me with suspicion, probably because I was wearing a tie and a business suit. But at least he listened to my pleas and promised some help.

I wondered who else I should talk to. Of course, the answer was the DLP, who at this time had six Senators in the Upper House, and had really strong influence on all decisions made by the Government. This led to their famous slogan "Keep the Bastards honest". I was ignorant of the political scene and knew nothing of the earlier bloodshed between the ALP and the DLP.

I made contact with the DLP, and there met the man who I still consider to be one of the finest ever that I have known in my life. This was Frank McManus, a man huge in both body and humanity. Frank listened to all I said, and he finally advised me to forget the Politicians, and to meet with the Unions, because that's where the real power existed.

I found that there were, like the parties themselves, Left Wing which tended towards the extremities of socialism, and Right Wing, which tended towards the more moderates. I am not going to become embroiled in the different politics, but I achieved my goal of meeting them all, and to explain what the CAG was trying to achieve in talking of the interests of everyday Australian.

In this process, we became quite interesting to the news hounds, and they regularly attended our meetings, and consequently we made several appearances on TV. At this time, the media had discovered that there existed in the UK a 'secret army' off right wing radicals who were dedicated to the destruction of socialism. The media in Australia were desperate to find a similar organisation here. Imagine the excitement when a particular Sunday paper found that I held a Commission in the RAN Reserve.

Immediately they produced an edition emblazoned with headlines "Dad's Army Exists in Australia."

We were quite active with public meetings and lecture tours, but the politics eventually won. The Prime Minister, Gough Whitlam was sacked and replaced by Malcom Fraser, a general election was held and the Labor Party was swept from power. The dust settled, but the arguments about all this have gone on over the years, and no doubt they will continue in the future, long after memories of those days are forgotten by most people.

Nevertheless, the main mission was accomplished, and soon after the Citizens' Action Group ceased to exist. It did however demonstrate how one person can start a land slide of opinion, and how keen is the media to have a story that they feel might increase their sales. If this is their motivation they may not bother to check how valid the background is before they publish.

45. Inaugral Melbourne to Hobart Yacht Race — 1972.

Life is strange — one never knows where it will take you. In the early 1970's, Lumacell Plastics pioneered the markets for expanded polystyrene sheet. We had captured a major share of the Australian pre-packed meat market with a range of food trays, and were test marketing laminated catering products.

However, we noted that South Africa had successfully used this material for a range of apple trays and these were used for their growing export field. At this time, apple packers in Australia used purple paper pulp trays.

Shipping was changing to the use of containers, and with apples the freight cost was based on the number of apple cases that could be packed into a standard container. The Victorian Research Centre at Scoresby realised that the cost of freight for apples could be reduced if the volume shipped in each container could be increased and this meant tightening the pack.

The cost of experimentation for the pulp tray manufacturer was prohibitive, considering the wide range of trays for the various sizes of apples, whereas for us it was simple. We simply cut the various sized fruit, nailed them on a board, took a plaster cast, and vacuum formed samples. The resultant modified pack became known as the "Scoresby Pack" and resulted in an increase in the number of cases per forty foot container by about twenty per cent.

A series of export trials were required, and these brought me into contact with Hedley Calvert, who ran Waterloo Packers in the Huon Valley, and exported about 900,000 cases of apples each year. He subsequently became a good friend. Although he was a very successful businessman, Hedley was at this time the leading ocean racing yacht skipper in Tasmania, and owned a famous yacht called "Huon Lass." He announced that he would enter the new Melbourne to Hobart ocean race instead of the usual Sydney to Hobart race.

About four days before Christmas 1972, Hedley and his crew arrived in "Huon Lass" at Hobsons Bay Yacht Club, but without their navigator who had arranged to fly to Melbourne on Christmas evening, so that he could spend that day with his family.

We had a couple of pleasant evenings with Hedley and his crew, and invited them to spend Christmas Day with my family. This was declined, on the grounds that they did not want to disturb our family celebrations. As it turned out, Christmas morning was cold and miserable, and very early I had a depressed Hedley on the phone asking if the invitation was still open. Taxis were quickly arranged and we had seven extra for lunch that day. They stayed until about four, and then sailed that evening to Queenscliff, where the race would start the next morning.

It was about 7pm Christmas night when I received another phone call from Hedley, saying that the Navigator had missed the plane he was expected to fly on, and the earliest he would arrive at Tullamarine would be the next morning, a little more than an hour before the race was due to start at Queenscliff. Hedley was depressed, because he felt he would have to cancel racing, being without his right-hand man. I told him I would see what I could do to help. It seemed impossible, especially being Christmas Day, with everything and everybody closed or relaxed.

I rang a colleague at the Aero Club for advice. He gave me the name and number of an aviator who ran a small hire plane business, though he did not really have much hope that this man could help me.

As luck would have it, not only did he answer the phone, but said that he would meet the Hobart plane the next morning and fly the person to a small airfield near Queenscliff. He gave detailed instructions as to how to find him and his plane at Tullamarine Airport.

So far so good, but our friend was still not in Queenscliff.

It so happens that because of the frequency of sailing at the Heads, I had made radio friends with the Lighthouse Keeper at Point Lonsdale. Nothing ventured, I found his home number, and again good fortune indeed smiled. He was home and full of Christmas cheer.

I asked him if he knew of a reliable local taxi driver, and he gave me a name and a number. Again, I was lucky and booked that taxi to meet a light aircraft at Barwon Heads airfield, and to drive the passenger quickly to the pier at Queenscliff.

All these arrangements were relayed to Hedley, who in turn contacted the navigator in Hobart and gave him all the necessary instructions. I doubt that any of us slept that night — there was so much that could go wrong.

The next morning it all worked like clock-work and the navigator was aboard the "Huon Lass" in time for the race to start. Surely, all this could only happen in Australia.

A few weeks later, I received a very generous picnic set from Hedley and the boys, with a note of thanks addressed to the "Maker of Miracles".

This was no miracle. I was just lucky to have friends and to know people who could help.

46. In Jordan for the United Nations

It all started with a realisation that the company I had started, to pioneer foam-plastic packaging trays was becoming too big for the existing premises at Moorabbin. We had already expanded enough to take over nearly the whole block.

This realisation was combined with the then policy of the State Government towards de-centralisation. In this policy, cheap land was available in country areas for businesses to accept incentives and to move their operation from metropolitan areas. Although predominately designed for country areas there were a few pockets fairly lose to Melbourne, such as Gisborne, Seymour, and Kilmore. It was decided that we should look closely at Kilmore, mainly because of its proximity to Melbourne.

When we spoke of our interest to the State Government, we were put in touch with a firm of consulting engineers, and a more detailed examination of our needs began. A close relationship with these people also resulted, and as a result, my own growing boredom with 'little white meat trays' became known.

It was resolved that the move to Kilmore was not viable, and alternative local premises were found. However, my new relationship was sustained, and sometime later I was approached with the suggestion that I should join their team as an adviser to the United Nations Development Program based in Amman, Jordan. This task was to find means of creating an economy for Jordan following the occupation of most of the productive areas of Jordan by Israel in the most recent conflict. My role was mainly to be marketing and to investigate the opportunities for a plastics industry in Jordan.

This sounded like the opportunity I was looking for. I resigned from Lumacell, and sold my shares back to Mulfords, the parent company, and started again a new phase of my life.

I can remember flying to Rome, and there being subjected to vigorous searching, which I did not mind at all. This was at the height of the Arab terrorist campaign and when looking at the dubious crowd of fellow passengers I was highly nervous and really quite relieved that there was such tight security.

Eventually we took off for Amman, and as we gained height I was nervously waiting for the "altitude bomb" to explode. At last we safely levelled off and I breathed again, to enjoy the sunshine and lovely food that Royal Jordanian Airways provided us with. The weather was perfect, and the views of the Greek Islands were so beautiful, sitting in

46. In Jordan for the United Nations

the sunshine like 'jewels in an azure sea.'

On arrival at Amman, I found there was already quite a team of mixed Australian and British experts of both sexes, plus a well — established office, manned mainly by westernised Arab girls. I was also introduced to three Bedouin young men, who were all graduates in economics from either British or American universities and who would work with me to identify the opportunity for a Jordan plastics industry.

I was given a Report made earlier by American consultants who had suggested that a facility be created for the manufacture of a range of plastics raw materials. This involved a huge financial investment with very few jobs created, and was obviously not an ideal solution for a country without any oil. I later realised that the first priority for a consultant was to recommend further involvement for themselves, and not necessarily a successful outcome for their client.

A further study also revealed that all the surrounding oil-producing nations, particularly in the Gulf States, had intentions to produce large volumes of various plastics raw materials, and to compete with them could not be viable, especially for a country like Jordan that had no oil to extract. Instead, the market would become highly competitive and inevitably the opportunity to negotiate low cost raw material supply would become obvious.

The first step was to learn about the existing market;

what were the opportunities for import replacement, what equipment was already available and what would be needed, and what allied services existed or had to be developed, such as engineers and tool makers for instance.

This study revealed that no extrusion equipment was operated and though there were a few blow and injection moulding machines installed, most plastics products were imported, and that local production was confined to a few plastic bottles and the like. All sorts of opportunities therefore existed for local production to replace imports.

Finance was readily available from Lebanese sources because of warfare that country and their businesses were looking to relocate in Jordan, though an important and restricting factor was the lack of technicians and trained staff within Jordan.

The way ahead became obvious. The marketing opportunities were identified, as were the variable sources of competitive raw materials. The needed secondary manufacturing equipment was identified, and the training of manpower in all areas of support was indicated to the Government.

The keynote was import replacement, and thereafter for exports of products and skilled labour, which would produce an indirect source of income for Jordan

My initial Report took some time to be researched but was eventually delivered to the King's brother, Prince Hussein. This royal Prince doubled as the Minister of Industry, and it was to him I reported.

The basis of my overall concept was the creation in Jordan of an industry similar to that which existed then in Hong Kong, where a multitude of small operators, mainly equipped with vacuum formers and injection moulding machines, together created a major contribution to that nation's economy. It would be a long job, starting from scratch, but with the right cooperation and finance from Government, a very worthwhile outcome could be anticipated and the effect on the Nation's economy by import s being replaced by local manufacture was obvious.

It was encouraging that Prince Hussein joined me in launching the Plastics Institute of Jordan. Among the first steps taken was to initiate a technical education unit for the training of necessary manpower. This meant official support in recruitment for education, and subsidised training overseas so necessary personnel would be ready.

This also included State subsidies for equipment, including items such as premises, toolmaking, and other ancillaries. For a while I felt part of a nationwide expansion.

The longer term results anticipated a trained core of personnel available for local and regional employment, import replacement, and a viable plastics industry, with a high ratio of employment against capital investment.

Eventually, I had fulfilled my task in planning the future and was impatient to return to Melbourne and to see my young family. Consequently I turned down many offers of employment, or vast sums of money as a lobbyist resulting from my relationships with those in power.

Money has never been my main motivation, but I did feel sad for departing from the close friends I had made among the many Jordanians, and Lebanese people I had met, and also from the others of our consulting team, whose work was not completed.

I had probably been more supportive to the Israeli side in my opinions previously. However, my time in Jordan, my friendships with the Arab people, and a growing admiration for their ethics, meant that I realized that there were two sides to the question.

We had spent many weekends in Jerusalem, and seeing first-hand the arrogance of young Israelis towards their Arab citizens only endorsed these new opinions.

Eventually, this interesting and rewarding time came to an end, and it has since been a source of reflection when my life returned to day to day normality. I was offered a similar job afterwards in the Philippines, but refused it, because the opportunity to return to my original maritime interest at the Polly Woodside arose.

Experiences and Life in Jordan.

I suppose the first surprise to me was the climate. For all my experience of the coldness of the Suez Canal in winter, I was taken by surprise by the low temperatures during the winter in Amman. First discovery was a lack of warm clothes, and then the answer to my complaint about the lack of a refrigerator in my room being "Just leave any beer bottles outside your window overnight."

My next surprise was the fact that alcoholic drinks were available in hotels and cafes. Life in Jordan was quite liberal and westernised compared to other Arab places, and this covered dress as well.

Jordan is made up of a mixture of religions, all tolerated, and retail shops were open according to the faith of the owner. Islamic owners closed on Fridays, Jewish on Saturdays, and Christian on Sundays.

Amman was originally the ancient Roman city of Philadelphia so the main interest is in the Roman ruins, including some famous bathhouses, which indicated that Jordan had once been a green and fertile land,

Roman ruins in Amman.

'The Treasury' — the hidden city of Petra in Jordan.

One of the most famous places is the hidden city of Petra, only re-discovered in the last century. To reach the ancient City, one had to mount horses and transit a narrow pebbly passage through high rocky cliffs.(On a recent TV show I saw that this passage is now paved.) This pathway is called the Syk. Eventually this leads to a magnificent carved structure called the Treasury, though this is actually only one of many Tombs throughout the old city area. There are even the ruins of an ancient Roman amphitheatre.

The carvings in the sandstone cliff was dated from the early Animite people, when the city was founded as a base in an ancient trading network. It was then added to by the Greeks, and then finally finished by the Romans. The water supply alone is a wonder of engineering.

Petra is now a tourist 'goldmine', and it fame and wonder been as exploited by its use as a film location.

An Amazing Sequel.

When I completed my work in Jordan I had a few days to spare before an appointment in Rome, so I decided to spend a weekend in Athens. On the flight from Amman to Athens I became friends with an ex-RAF type, who had at one stage been active in training pilots for the Jordan Air Force, and had then set up a company manufacturing prefabricated housing for the Middle East oil industry. His company was based in Greece just outside Athens.

Because of our new friendship, he offered me hospitality in Athens. He showed me all the sights of the City, culminating in a fabulous family Sunday lunch at a City hotel prior to leaving Athens that afternoon.

Some will remember that at that time, nearly all the taxi drivers in Melbourne were of Greek nationality. It happened inevitably that our Sunday lunch went longer than planned, and regretfully I tore myself apart from my new-found friends, ran quickly down the hotel steps, and hailed a Taxi.

I explained to the driver in something akin to 'pidgeon English' that I needed to get to the Airport quickly.

Imagine my surprise when I was answered by a broad Australian voice speaking the familiar words — "She'll be right, mate" The driver was from Melbourne, on a working holiday and driving a cab for his uncle.!

47. My trip as a Tourist to South America.

It all started at a usual Saturday lunchtime gathering at the Yacht Club bar.

One of my friends asked me if I had ever sailed round Cape Horn, and I had to admit that although I had been to most parts of the world, either as a seafarer or on business, I had never been to any part of South America, other than the Panama Canal.

It was in the Christmas period of 2005, the schools were on holiday, and I had recently been divorced. My friend, the late Ron Botica, had been widowed and he was very depressed. He admitted that he had asked the question because he had read an advertisement about a cruise to the area. This was aboard the cruise ship the 'Norwegian Crown'.

I had never been a passenger before and I found the idea appealing. The timing meant I could get away, the cost, including airfares, was reasonable, so Ron and I decided to go.

We flew to Santiago, the capital city of Chile, and after two days of sightseeing, including a visit to a winery, then to Rio, we joined the ship in Valparaiso. I remember that soon

Santiago, Chile

after we sailed, I received a mobile phone call from my son, Nick, sailing my yacht on Port Phillip in Melbourne, asking for advice because the steering gear had broken. I was able to advise him. Modern communications are wonderful.

During this tour of South America we visited many small communities, each of which seemed to be based on the European country from which the original settlers came from. We found that the country of Chile, being long and narrow and stretching from near the Equator to the coldest and mountainous South, was very Latitudinal and the regional economy of each varied according to the local climate. The variations included the mining of ores, wine

47. My trip as a Tourist to South America.

growing, lamb breeding, and other suitable forms of agriculture from North to South. The land includes dry deserts and mountainous glaciers.

Before the construction of the Panama Canal in the early twentieth century, the only route from Europe to the Pacific or to the Gold Fields of California was to circumnavigate the whole continent and weather the fearsome Cape Horn against the funnelled Westerly winds. Sailing ships trading to Australia would choose to sail with these winds behind them, coming to Australia via South Africa and homeward bound to Europe via the frightful Cape Horn with a following wind.

Thanks to the famous voyage of H.M.S. Beagle, the infamous Cape Horn could be by-passed by ships using the Magellan Straits, and it was part of the route we followed,

Photograph taken while rounding Cape Horn.

this including many glaciers among the mountains of the region. I was amazed at how the sailing ships, without engines, ever navigated this route.

Both Ron and I were strong fans of the Chilean wines, and during this visit we learnt that the favourite red wine known as Carmanere was originally a form of Merlot from France, but escaped the disease in France that wiped out the whole region, by being on a ship bound for Chile. Most of the current Chilean wine growers were using Australian or New Zealand technology.

We were amused by watching the European waitresses aboard the ship struggling to open modern screw top Chilean wines with a cork-screw. This was a form of sealing that had not been adopted yet in Europe.

Typical view of Magellan Straits, Sth.America.

47. My trip as a Tourist to South America.

The trip include a transit of the Magellan Straits, a circumnavigation of Cape Horn, a visit to the Falkland Islands , which were proudly British after their recovery from the Argentine invasion, and then to Rio and Buenos Aires.

We found that because if the annual festival at Rio there was no way hotel bookings could be made for us according to the schedule, so to keep faith the tour company flew us a no cost to Rio before the ship sailed from Santiago. This gesture was much appreciated.

I had not been aboard any ship for many years previous to this trip, and was anxious to visit the Bridge. On my request for this at the Purser's desk I was told that since the Nine Eleven event such visits were not allowed. However, it so happened on that very day I bumped onto the Norwegian Captain and after I explained my professional background,

Picture of Stanley in Falklands. (Very British)

he invited me to visit the wheel house at any time. I learnt that during the voyage, we carried both Chilean and Argentinian pilots, who worked their respective areas. Apparently, both these countries had recently come close to war because of disputed lands, an event only avoided by the personal intervention of the Pope. These two pilots worked in close harmony and were both welcoming to a member of the cloth.

All in all, I enjoyed the experience of being a tourist and was pleased that I had taken the opportunity. The passengers aboard this ship were mainly from Britain of Germany, and our Southern skies were unknown to them. I entertained large groups each evening after dinner by giving short courses on our local Astronomy.

Among these passenger was Frank Blakeway and his wife. Frank, who has remained as a friend since then, was a previous President of the Royal Cartographical Association, and who arranged my subsequent visit to the RN Hydrographic office in Devon, to view the original charts of Australia by Cook and Flinders. That was a highlight in my career as a maritime museum Director in Melbourne.

Footnote

I mentioned at the start of this section that I had never before visited South America. The closest I had ever been was on the Great Circle track from Wellington to Panama, passing close to Easter Island with its famous stone statues.

47. My trip as a Tourist to South America.

During one such voyage, on a dark and stormy southern ocean night, through the gloom appeared the lights of what appeared to be an ordinary cargo ship. Being a passenger ship, we were lit up like a Christmas Tree.

The usual Morse lamp exchange of signals took place — "What ship?" and "Where bound?— and then suddenly her light started sending a new signal. "We'll swop you two cases of beer for two virgins."

I had to think quickly, and sent back "You are too late!"

48. My time at the Polly Woodside

It was after I returned to Melbourne from a period of working for the United Nations in Jordan that I responded to an invitation to join the restoration of the sailing vessel Polly Woodside, which had for years been employed as the coal hulk 'Rona.'

When I first joined the team at the Polly Woodside, there was still the original group that had undertaken the task of restoration. The ship and premises were the property of the National Trust of Victoria. The local Committee, to whom I reported, was guided by the local Chairman, Mr John Yunken, and was responsible to the National Trust's Directors.

I found that the local Committee, all volunteers, referred to themselves as the 'Ship Committee' and were pretty jealous of the total restoration of the ship, as opposed to the general activities of the project as a whole. This included the embryo Maritime Museum, although the collection of artefacts had already begun, as had an initial campaign for raising funds.

The Chairman, being an architect, had re-designed the

whole site, which had been for years the previous Duke & Orr dry dock, and donated by the then Premier, Sir Rupert Hamer, to the National Trust as a permanent home for the ship. The previous dock facilities and buildings were given to house the embryo Melbourne Maritime Museum. The whole site was thus actually on designated Crown Land.

From the outset it became obvious that my activities, based on generally raising the profile of the place, and to increase its viability, were viewed as worthwhile, as long as I did nothing initially to change the use or appearance of the ship itself.

The ship was an interesting reminder of the way Melbourne developed, but I felt that in itself it meant nothing in an educational sense unless the whole world of maritime life and culture was included.

My initial efforts included making the place a general meeting place of all those bodies that had an interested in

Polly Woodside's site between Wars.

48. My time at the Polly Woodside

ships, and a great many associations accepted the invitation to adopt the place as their headquarters. These organisations also became a great recruiting ground for volunteers. I also realised quite early that the only 'all year' visitor market was the schools, especially for the Monday to Friday markets.

Consequently I quickly formed the volunteer Education Committee, made up of mainly school teachers who willingly gave their efforts and time without reward.

These wonderful people produced educational books about ships, life at sea, and the early days of our seaport. They also produced a card game of Nautical Happy Families, and all these items are still available. Notable was the creation of a Sound and Light Show, a great favourite with the schools until all the control equipment was stolen one night. This had been set up in a mock-up migrant ship hull that I bludged from the Education Department following an exhibit they produced at the Royal Show, and housed in a restored cargo shed at the rear of the property.

A special event was the light opera, "HMS Pinafore" held aboard Polly Woodside, with audience stands erected alongside. This starred John English, and we were lucky with the weather as it was a sell out for ten days. This was followed by a special drama based on the famous Mutiny on the Bounty and performed by Art students for a week.

The original snack bar that we called "Greasy Joes" made from a shipping container, was replaced with a specially constructed function centre. This served lunches and snacks for visitors, and also held many events, dinners, fashion shows, and club nights.

The room originally used as an Art Gallery was used as a meeting room for a variety of Associations which I encouraged to use the Museum as their Headquarters. It also became a lecture room for schools, and was fitted with a large TV, donated by the Young Trust.

My biggest problem was the lack of funds. We had no grants from the State, and the Trust had little money to share around the many properties for which they were responsible. Consequently, I had to become the greatest of "bludgers", or beggars, to obtain rope, steel, tools, and even the anodes to protect the hull. When the volunteers were

Ship's Birthday — from left — Johnny Young, John Bertrand, C.T., and Michael Parker.

48. My time at the Polly Woodside

unable to continue with a job because of a lack of material, my powers of persuasion came to the fore.

I had only a small staff, two girls who doubled their office work by guiding school tours, a male hand for general maintenance, and above all, Tor Linquist, who was an experienced sailor and who was really responsible for the re-rigging of the ship.

All tasks were done by a huge gang of dedicated volunteers, who not only worked aboard the ship and acted as Guides, but ran the souvenir shop, cleaned the embryo museum, and looked after the grounds. Prominent were the members from the Seamens' Union, my old sparing partners, who I learnt to respect whole heartedly. They themselves were doubtful about me as first, with my background as a ship's Chief Officer, but we all got along well.

I have written below a few detailed accounts of other events that we enjoyed during my years running Melbourne's 'Tall Ship', but it is too difficult to list them all — we had so many. The monthly 'Family Days' are still held, and these would include a particular attraction like the RAN Band or the celebrated Pirates' Day; the special Thursday school events with Sea Shanty concerts, shipboard games, and cooking maritime meals in the ship's galley (to the horror of many of the early ship oriented volunteers.)

It was during this time that the Committee agreed with my suggestion that we should construct a replica of the schooner "Enterprize", the ship that actually could be said to founding Melbourne in 1835, and a sub-committee was formed and the first finance was raised. (Details of this project are in the next chapter.)

Some Memories from years at the Polly Woodside.

1. The Ash Tray.

I had advertised for a female Guide, to help with the school tours of the Polly Woodside, preferably with some first aid experience. Among the applicants was a charming Belgian lady.

Rita had been a Nursing Sister aboard the Belgian passenger ships running from Antwerp to Matardi in the Belgian Congo, and I remembered that while we were loading cargo in Matardi, we used to go aboard the Belgian passenger ship "Brazzaville" to enjoy the air conditioning and to have the odd cold beer.

Polly's whaler rigged as Barque.

48. My time at the Polly Woodside

Matartdi is about sixty miles up the fast flowing Congo River. It is a very hot and steamy City. It was always a pleasure to get away from our ship while we were loading, and to visit the 'Brazzaville' with its air conditioned lounges. This was actually a replacement haven after the Elder Dempster passenger ship "Accra" had sailed.

We first chose to drink beer aboard "Accra" because we were welcomed into the Second Engineer's cabin. He had tapped the cold beer pipe to the Passenger's Bar that ran through his wardrobe, meaning we had low-cost refreshment.

During one of our sessions aboard the "Brazzaville", I had 'purloined' one of the ship's ash trays, with the name of the shipping Line printed on it — "Messageres Maritime". That trophy had since been lost.

In the course of the interview, I discovered that Rita and her husband, who had set up a sales office in the Congo, had only just escaped the slaughter of Europeans when Congo achieved independence from the Belgians. In the conversation, I also mentioned the story about stealing the ash tray.

I met other applicants that day and the winner was to be decided later, but Rita was always the front runner

When I arrived at work the next morning, I found a blue Messageres Maritime ash tray, identical to the one I had stolen so many years previously, sitting on my desk.

Rita got the job!

2. The Labour Day Fireworks Display.

Every year over the Labour Weekend on the Monday, it was a local custom that a river pageant should be held prior to the evening display of fireworks. In that particular year, it was agreed that our ex-Navy whaler boat from the Polly Woodside wood lead the parade.

We fitted this boat to be a replica of Polly Woodside herself. Masts and spars were created from broomsticks and other suitable dowel timber, and the lady volunteers made a suit of sails for her. When fully rigged, the result was really quite impressive.

I had the good fortune to meet an executive from one of the participating fireworks companies and it was arranged that a pigeon- hole box of "Bangers" would be installed in the bow of the whaler, so that a twenty- gun salute could be fired between Swanson and Swan Bridges, in the way that a visiting warship would do.

To perform the marketing benefit for the Polly Woodside, an illuminated name box was fitted to provide identity, and this proved sufficient to raise cheers of support from the families watching the event from the riverbank.

The night of the event was fine with a moderate southerly wind. This was ideal for us, because this breeze was sufficient to propel the boat with its rig of sails at exactly the required speed, without having to rely upon the boat's engine.

A crew of about six had been dressed out as Nelsonian

48. My time at the Polly Woodside

sailors, complete with straw boater hats. The whole setup was pretty impressive, and we looked the part that we intended. The rest of the water pageant formed up behind us, and we all proceded though the City. Fortunately, it was low tide, and we just scraped under both the Spencer St, Bridge and also the old iron Railway Bridge, so all went well, until we approached the Swanson Street Bridge.

Standing on the bridge w ere a group of obviously patriotic but heavily intoxicated Aboriginal spectators. Associating our craft with those of the early British settlers of 1788 at Botany Bay, we were subjected to yells of "Go back to where you came from!" and other similar but less polite pleasantries , and we received a fusillade of beer cans, some still full. These were made pretty welcome, even though they hurt if we suffered a direct hit.

After this excitement, we sailed into area of the river where the southern riverside borders the Botanic Gardens. This is where the bulk of the spectators were sitting, so it was time to fire the Gun Salute. I made my way forward and lay down in the bows. I fired the first shot, and found that this had much greater power than I had first thought and the recoil dislodged the whole container. I had no option but to hold the whole contraption in place with one hand whilst firing the remaining shots.

This was extremely hazardous and I risked being burned. However, nothing very serious resulted, but I emerged without eyebrows, and some singed hair on my arms. Any remaining nervousness was more than compensated by the applause from the families on the shore, so at least the marketing aims had been achieved and we knew that the Polly Woodside was accepted and endorsed as a Melbourne icon.

Because we had added the masts, we could not get under the Swan Street Bridge, and had no option but to run the boat up on the southern bank grass. The rest of the procession past us by, and then sheltered at the far side of the bridge. We were left alone and in close proximity to the three barges moored in the river, each laden with the fireworks for the display and which were fired remotely from the shore.

When the show started, we realised how close to the action we were. There was really no danger, and with the deafening noise, it was actually quite exciting. We felt that we were involved as in a historical sea battle, and referred to it afterwards as being like witnessing the Battle of Trafalgar.

It was something rather of an anti-climax when the show finished, and the time came to start the motor, and make our way peacefully back to the Polly Woodside and home.

3. Celebrating the Arrival of the first Salmon and Trout spawn

The first successful arrival of salmon and brown trout spawn from the United Kingdom was aboard the sailing ship 'Norfolk in 1864. There had been earlier attempts, sponsored by homesick migrants, but the long and slow passages in those days before refrigeration, proved a barrier.

However, this successful shipment, carefully packed in insulated containers and combined with good fortune causing a speedy passage, meant that the ship 'Norfolk' arrived in Melbourne in April 1864 with the precious cargo alive and well. The packages were swiftly unloaded on to waiting horse drawn carts, and taken to the new Ice Works in South Melbourne. These were then distributed to places in Victoria, Tasmania, and later, New Zealand, and it was from these spawn that the game fisheries that exist throughout our nations today actually are originated.

To commemorate this event, a re-enactment was held aboard Polly Woodside, 125 years later, under the sponsorship of the Australian Trout Foundation. Among the guests was the President of the Foundation. Mr Terry George.

A commemoration plaque was riveted onto the Starboard bulwark by John Bertrand, famous as skipper of the yacht 'Australia 2' which had just won the America's Cup from the USA. Although shipyard people were in attendance, John insisted that he would do the task himself.

4. 1988 — Australia's Bi-Centennial Celebrations
The year 1988 saw Australia hold its Bi-Centennial, and a multitude of celebrations were held all over the country. From a maritime perspective the foremost event was a re-enactment of the voyage of the First Fleet. These original

eleven small ships initiated the European settlement of Australia.

This re-enactment was the brain child of Jonathon King and his father, descendants of the original Governor of Australia, and was a voyage of a mixed fleet of sailing ships from Portsmouth in England to Sydney, sailing the same route as the original Fleet 200 years previously. I was present to watch the departure of this re-enactment fleet from Portsmouth.

Their arrival in Sydney was triumphal, but not to be outdone, Melbourne later hosted a visit of International tall ships which were open for the public at Port Melbourne

Naturally, we wanted the Polly Woodside to be part of this, and two events were held. First was a rowing boat race. This was planned for crews from each of the ships to man in turn R.A.N. 27 foot whalers, but we had difficulty in locating even two such boats. Even then it was only last minute repair work by the good services of shipwright Tom Whitfield that made one such boat available. In the event ships were allowed to use any boat that they had available.

The course was parallel to Station Pier, and volunteer judges were appointed. I had persuaded the ANZ Bank to award a trophy, which was fittingly won by cadets from the new ship 'Young Endeavour', a Bi-centennial gift from the UK to Australia.

At the same time, our previous Gift Shop had been

transformed into an Art Gallery, and held a display of paintings that portrayed ships and events that had been experienced during the voyage to Australia by the re-enactment Fleet. These had been painted by the Fleet Artist during the voyage by the commissioned Artist, who was actually a Grandson of the famous writer Taylor Coleridge (Rhyme of the Ancient Mariner) and who afterwards married and settled in Australia.

5. The Voyage to mark the Polly Woodside's centennial
The ship was launched in Belfast in November 1885. On the approach of her 100th Birthday we knew we had to do something special to commemorate such a special day. A combined meeting of the Ship Committee and the Volunteers considered the options, but because of the ship's landlocked situation, these were limited.

We could hold a major ceremony aboard the ship, but this would limit the festivity and not be highly marketable. I felt that we had to do something that would attract all the media here and overseas, as well as getting the most publicity to the general public.

It was finally agreed that we should stage a Centennial Voyage, even though it could only mean taking the ship across the river to the World Trade Centre. This was a small trip compared with the long voyages the ship had achieved in her life, but at least it would prove to the World that she was still floating.

There were still a couple of hurdles to overcome. First, since the building of the Grimes Bridge, the dredgers were not able to work in our section of the river, and this was silting up fast. Soundings showed us that even at high water there would barely be enough water for even our shallow draught. However, the silt was really thin, soft mud, and even if our soundings were wrong, damage to the hull was unlikely and our transit would not be impeded.

An even bigger problem existed in providing the towage, the Polly Woodside having no engines herself. Again, this was because the construction of the Grimes Bridge was too low to allow any of the regular harbour tugs to enter our section of the river or to handle the ship.

A conference with the Port Authority provided the solution. Every possible motor launch and line-boat would be used, and it was felt these would be adequate, providing the weather was fine and the flow of the river minimised. The final point was covered by the Port Phillip Pilots supplying the necessary Pilot for the voyage, both to and from the World Trade Centre, and I should stress that all those that took part, whatever their task and including the crew aboard the ship provided by the Seamen's Union members, gave their services free of charge, thus allowing the event to take place without an otherwise financial burden.

Thanks to the publicity given to the event by the ABC public programmes and the local newspapers, the marketing was successful, and when Australia Post decided to open a Post Office aboard and to issue a special pre-stamped envelope for the commemoration, it proved to be a most worthwhile exercise. (Sample below)

We spent a week a t the World Trade Centre altogether before returning to the Dock. During this time the night security was provided by the local Sea Cadets who slept aboard and kept watches as if the ship was at sea.

I feel sure that the exercise, with attendant publicity, cemented the Polly Woodside in the hearts of the population as part of the Melbourne scene.

6. World Recognition of Polly Woodside in 1988
The greatest thrill of all the eleven years I spent as CEO of the Polly Woodside (also known as the coal hulk Rona at one stage) was the day the ship was awarded the Maritime Heritage Medal by the World Ship Trust. (Correctly titled

'The International Congress of Maritime Museums'.) This was medal Number Five, and the award was presented on the 17th October 1988.

Polly Woodside arrives at World Trade Center Centennial Voyage — November 1985

In winning this award, Polly Woodside joined the celebrated ranks of famous ships around the World — HMS Victory, the famous Cutty Sark, HMS Warrior, USS Constitution, and the previously sunken Swedish vessel "Vasa", all earlier winners of this form of recognition. By now, there are many more restored ships on the list, most notably the 'Mary Rose' with all its souvenirs of life in Elizabethan times.

However at that time we were in competition for medal Number Five with the Sydney based ship "James Craig" for it had been decided by the International Trust that one ship in Australia should be awarded the medal during the Australian Bi-Centennial year of 1988.

48. My time at the Polly Woodside

At the time of the decision, James Craig was in a bad way. She was perched precariously on a raft, and her old plates were being removed, leaving a bare skeleton of the fine ship that she is today. I had held correspondence with one of the World Ship Trustees that I had met during a previous visit and learnt of forth-coming decision in that way. I resolved that we would win that medal.

I was in London just before their final decision, and received an invitation to lunch with the Trustees. This was a pretty awesome occasion, dining with Lord this, and Sir something that. Worse still, the occasion was held at one of those "leather armchair" exclusive London clubs.

I prepared myself for the coming meeting. I stressed what a mess James Craig was in and how hopeless her future appeared. I really laid it on very thick, and presumably convincingly, because by the time that I was back in Melbourne it was announced that Polly Woodside would receive the award.

The Case for the Medal

A key event leading up to the actual presentation was the making of a case to hold the medal. I had received an inquiry from London asking if we had some timber from the original ship for the medal case to be made from, because they had craftsmen who could do the job.

As part of the restoration of the ship, we had renewed

a length of the original pin rail, and this wood was available. I had two pieces perhaps 12 inches square by three inches thick prepared. These were made of teak, and the weight was unimaginable. The next problem was getting these heavy chunks of wood to London without the National Trust going bankrupt in the process.

At this same time, my ex-wife Tracy Watt was Art Director for a joint British-Australian movie production called "The Four Minute Mile", and the Brits has sent out their film Director, Jim Goddard for the filming. We entertained Jim quite a bit while he was here, took him out sailing, wined and dined him, etc. and finally had lunch with him before he went out to Tullamarine to catch his London bound plane. He was a great guest and a lovely man.

I can remember saying to him "Would you mind taking two pieces of wood as hand baggage", knowing that he could hardly refuse. I had them in the car with us, and only in the process of passing them to him did he realise how heavy the favour was. He took them as baggage for the trip to London in fine spirit, never the less.

The medal itself was cast in gun metal and was a thing of beauty, but the box that was made from the timber we sent was incredible. The craftsmanship displayed was a realisation that real skills still exist to this day.

The whole parcel was sent out some time before the actual event — in time for me to make some silicon rubber copies. **(Just as well, because I have learnt that the real Medal** has since been "lost", and the present whereabouts of the crafted wooden case is unknown.)

The Presentation Ceremony.

The Chairman of the Polly Woodside at the time was the late Commander Michael Parker, RN. Rtd., who had been previously ADC to the Duke of Edinburgh. Michael entered into the spirit of the day with unleashed enthusiasm, especially when he learnt that our big day coincided with a visit to Melbourne by the aircraft carrier HMS Ark Royal.

Because the Brits would not say if the ship carried nuclear weapons or not, she was not allowed to berth in Melbourne, but spent her visit here circling Port Phillip Bay. Michael's idea of having the medal delivered by Harrier Jet was knocked back on the grounds of community safety, but his perseverance meant that we would have the wonderful Royal Marine band from the ship, flown ashore to play at the event.

The actual presentation was made by the then State Governor, Dr David McCaughey, before an audience of Dignitaries, the Directors of the National Trust, the Polly Woodside Volunteers, and invited Guests, with all being entertained by the wonderful band of the Royal Marines.

All went well. It was truly a day to remember, a day that was properly dedicated to the hundreds of volunteers who made possible the restoration of that scruffy coal hulk to the fine ship she is today and in acknowledging that the National Trust had the courage to undertake the job. They had actually purchased the ship, as a coal hulk, from Howard Smith Ltd. for the sum of One Cent, and as a result they gave the City of Melbourne and Australia the icon that today holds completely the memory of the birth of modern Australia.

Sequels — Why do I remember the date? I must be one of the few people in the World who had the "Happy Birthday Song" played for them by a Band of the Royal Marines because it was on my birthday, the 17th October 1988.

I should also mention that our accountant at the time was Cathy Campbell — a real live and typical Aussie girl. I remember turning up in my Chief Officer's rig from earlier days, to be greeted by Cathy with raised eyebrows and some appropriate sarcastic remark. I defended myself by saying that I had purchased that uniform in Valetta way back in the 1960's. Cathy came back with the quick rejoinder "You must have been a fat slob even then". It was an unforgettable and perfect squelch.

An Enduring Icon for Melbourne and Australia.

I am proud of those years and what together we achieved. It certainly was not measured in terms of financial reward, but we all felt the glow of achievement in what we had together created for the Melbourne community.

The View from 2020

Penniless Cadets and the Mission

By Jay Miller

In September this year, Chief Manager Sue Dight was delighted to hear from a seafaring cadet of yesteryear. Mr Charles Treleaven of Williamstown and now aged 87, has strong memories of the warm hospitality that was offered to penniless cadets in the 1950s by various branches of the Mission to Seafarers in Williamstown, Geelong and here at the Melbourne Mission on Flinders Street.

As Charles recalls "It was during this time I discovered the delights and hospitality of the Mission...I have such happy memories of the Flying Angel Clubs...really home away from home for us broke cadets...and we are still thankful for the skills learned playing ping-pong and billiards."

Charles worked aboard the British ship the *SS Saint Gregory*. Built during wartime and then commissioned to bring coal from Calcutta to Melbourne during the strikes of 1950, it then discharged it at the Gas Works formerly off Flinders St Extension. On the same trip they loaded coal fuel bunkers from a coal hulk called the *Rona*.

Charles in later years went on to make a significant contribution to the maritime history of Melbourne. "Little did I realise that in later years I would become a CEO and lead the restoration of the vessel *Rona* which we now know today with her original name as the *Polly Woodside*". Moored just across from the Mission, on the River Yarra, the *Polly Woodside* regularly undergoes maintenance carried out by a devoted team of volunteers and is owned by the National Trust of Australia.

The preservation of these two significant historic features on the south and north banks of the river – both linked by the contemporary Seafarers Bridge - are important repositories of memories for so many people like Charles and the dedicated workers and volunteers of the Flying Angel Club and the Mission, who have added to the maritime heritage of the area throughout the 20th and 21st centuries.

Polly Woodside

We will ensure that Charles' memories are preserved in our Heritage Archive together with the images featured here. Many thanks Charles!

If you have memories and stories of the Mission to Seafarers or your time at sea to share, the Heritage team would love to hear from you info@missiontoseafarers.com.au

page 9

335

I believe that my indignation towards Victorian politicians of either Party who would boast about the creation of such an icon for Australia is more than justified. When they would say "Look what we have done in restoring the Polly Woodside", I would answer "You did absolutely nothing compared to the Volunteers!" The exception to this was Sir Rupert Hamer who gave us the dry dock site, when he was Premier of Victoria, supposedly in perpetuity, although this was by-passed by Jeff Kennett when he built "Jeff's Shed" later.

After so much achievement, but with so many non-players claiming their part in the success that followed, I became disillusioned and somewhat depressed. I was reminded of my position by the words of my then wife — "You don't need all this nonsense, Charlie." and I resolved to leave, and to start my own business.

My interest in Melbourne's maritime background led to the foundation of the Maritime Heritage Association of Victoria. (MHAV). This was another attempt to mark the memory of the Victoria's long connection with the sea. (Details about the MHAV are in chapter 50.)

49. The Replica of Schooner 'Enterprize'. (Including a Sequel)

At the time that the Enterprize project was born, there were massive changes taking place at the Polly Woodside, and to a high degree I found some of the new direction confusing. The original management committee had really been relegated as the 'Ship Committee' and the main energy of the Chairman and the General Committee was now directed towards making the Polly Woodside totally independent from the National Trust. I knew that there were several legal hurdles to make such a move impossible, but the Chairman, Cmdr. Parker, felt he could overcome them.

As CEO of the project, I continued with my marketing efforts to achieve viability, though I found the attitude towards my systems of measuring financial control in favour of a so called more 'big business' approach very frustrating, because of the delay in producing figures to gauge actual progress.

We had previously agreed to build the two ship's boats for the Polly Woodside, and the tasks had been assigned to two shipwrights, Arthur Woodley and Tom Whitfield. This work was proceeding at this time.

Also on the General Committee was Hedley Elliot. Hedley was owner of the reception rooms at Emu Bottom, a property actually leased originally by George Evans, who had been aboard Faulkner's ship 'Enterprize' when it was the first ship to start the Melbourne settlement by Europeans on 30th August 1835. This was also actually Melbourne's first pre-fabricated house. This date was commemorated as the birthday of Melbourne.

Because of this connection, Hedley had initiated an annual event as Melbourne's birthday, held annually at the location of Enterprize's berth on South Bank. (After the construction of the Enterprize replica this site was occupied by the steel sculpture, known as The Vault — though more commonly known as the Yellow Peril — and which thereafter provided a venue for graffiti and a shelter for the Homeless.)

At a later Board meeting, my suggestion that our shipwrights could build a replica of the Enterprize was well received, and I was instructed to form a Committee to study the feasibility, and also to try to raise the funds required to at least provide the initial working drawings of the ship. Of the two shipwrights involved, Tom Whitfield declared his pleasure to participate.

Accompanied by Tom, together we raised $10,000 from each of the City of Melbourne and the Museum of Victoria, who both declared their interest in the heritage project.

With these funds, the initial plans were commissioned and later obtained from Karl Markhardt, a naval architect.

Eventually, and just prior to my resignation from Polly Woodside, the keel of the ship was laid, with baulks of donated timber. Apparently, sometime later the floundering project was rescued financially by a wealthy sponsor and the ship was eventually launched on 30th August 1997 at Williamstown, Victoria, by Mrs Kennett, wife of the then Premier of Victoria. It was exactly on the City's 162nd Birthday. Following the launching, the Enterprize proceeded upstream to Victoria Dock.

I escorted her in my yacht, while Tom Whitfield was on board the Enterprize. At some stage of this voyage, Tom called out to me "Look what we started, Charley !"

Replica — ship "Enterprize"

The earlier dream of a replica of the ship that founded the City of Melbourne had been created.

There are not many cities in the world that can observe their actual dates of foundation. The site of the City was decided by discovery of fresh water above the waterfall located just upstream of what became Prince's Bridge (Previously called the Falls Bridge) This blocked the pollution of tidal salt water in the lower river stream.

An amusing sequel

The Polly Woodside's Chairman at the time was the late Michael Parker who had previously been ADC to Prince Phillip Mountbatten. While in this role, he and the Prince had been involved in saving the clipper ship, Cutty Sark, as a symbol of Britain's maritime heritage.

With this background, Michael suggested that the Governor of Victoria should be asked to become a Patron of the Enterprize project, and accordingly I made the appointment with His Excellency.

Three of us, Michael Parker, Hedley Elliot, and I arrived at Government House, with Hedley carrying an framed etching of the original Enterprize when tied up at South Bank. This picture was wrapped in brown paper and was to be presented to the Governor.

We were greeted at the door by a female ADC, who suggested that the brown paper should be removed before the presentation. After this was done, we saw Hedley's face go pale. Instead of a picture of Enterprize, there was a painting of a Victorian girl cuddling a fluffy cat. (I suspect the substitution was the action of Jane Elliot)

Nonplussed, the ADC took this revelation in her stride, and came up with a classic remark — "Well!" she said, "We thought we were getting a picture of a Bark, but instead we have a Miaow !"

Commemoration Medals

Not long after the launching of the replica ship, the Members of the original Foundation committee were issued with a medal, recognising their part in marking this historic event. This was in the form of granting a Rite of Passage aboard the ship. A picture of this historic medal is attached below.

It is interesting that many years later, the then Manager of the Enterprize Foundation and in charge of the ship's operations, knew nothing of these medals and this story of the ship's creation.

The Enterprize Medal

Apparently the privileges granted by this award are hereditary and can be extended to any subsequent offspring.

50. The Maritime Heritage Association of Victoria, (MHAV)

The years at the Polly Woodside had created a new interest for me. I had always been interested in history, but these years had shown me that while Australia had been born of the sea, most Australians as a whole were singularly ignorant of the part played in the development of the Nation by ships and sailors, and the history of such all over world. This was true particularly in Victoria, where there is much more interest in the Bush, than in the ships that brought them and their forebears here.

Various bodies have endeavoured to tell stories of their local events, and have set up small museums to tell these stories, but there was nobody in Melbourne to teach the whole background to seafaring, which includes so many subjects, like Astronomy, Shipbuilding, Stability, Cargoes, Migration, etc. In Victoria there is a no State maritime museum as in all other States, while a National Maritime Museum has been set up in Sydney.

(The trade-off was to be a National Aeronautical Museum

in Melbourne but this has never happened to date, as far as I know)

At the same time, the National Trust was suffering from a lack of funds and had threatened to shut down the Polly Woodside operation. This was well after my departure, but my interests were still alive, and I resolved that this would not happen.

I called a general meeting, and was amazed at the enormous response, which indicated vast interest in ships and the sea among the general public, as it was among the various maritime interest Groups that had adopted the Museum.

As a result a properly constituted body was later formed, and duly registered as the "Maritime Heritage Association of Victoria." The registration was dated 16th September 2002. A Constitution was drawn up, and a Committee was elected which nominated the main Aims and Objectives of the Association. Membership was made up by a mixture of various maritime oriented bodies and private citizens.

We were also very proud to announce that Sir Rupert Hamer, the previous Premier of Victoria had agreed to become our Patron. Sir Rupert, now deceased, had always shown himself to be interested in the maritime heritage of Victoria. It was he who gave the State owned ex-Dry Dock site as the home for the Polly Woodside.

With thanks to Kate Lance a website was established, (mhav.net) and although the Association has been long gone,

50. The Maritime Heritage Association of Victoria, (MHAV)

this may still be seen, and the early newsletters still read, which track the early activities of the MHAV.

The main objectives of the Association were to increase the knowledge and appreciation of our maritime history among Australians generally, and to see created a State Maritime Museum, which was lacking in Victoria, compared with other States. The marine sciences and their evolution is an important item and mainly ignored by existing regional Museums.

It was agreed that to achieve the first objective, emphasis should be placed on the Education of all ages, by a range of printed booklets, by public presentations and slide shows, and encouragement to visit the embryo Maritime Museum at the Polly Woodside. The icon for this was the Polly Woodside itself, and to promote tours of the Port of Melbourne and the River Yarra, which has many items of maritime history.

In an effort to achieve the objective of a State Maritime Museum was a campaign to promote the concept among politicians, and to search for a suitable site, with an emphasis on a location that was within reach of the population of Melbourne itself.

In the first place, the work instituted by the Polly Woodside's education committee was to be expanded, though already the volume of schools visiting was encouraging. This work was added to by training of skippers of tourist boats plying the River Yarra, and researching the history of the Port.

Plans were made to link by water the various sites of nautical background along the River Yarra, including The Aquarium, The Polly Woodside, the Flying Angel, the Science Museum, HMAS Castlemaine, and terminating at Seaworks in Williamstown.

It became obvious the main ethos of the population was with the bush and the gold rush period, and people were unaware of the size and tonnage handled by the Port. It was unlike Sydney, where everybody saw the ships and the Harbour. Just about everybody who did a trip from the City down to Williamstown remarked afterwards that they had no idea of the size and nature of the Port of Melbourne.

Changing the public attitude to maritime affairs was an obvious necessity, if the assistance of politicians was to be gained. Politicians need to know that votes are involved. The support of the City of Melbourne given to the Polly Woodside was not to be counted on if the chosen site was outside the area controlled by the Council.

Several sites around Melbourne, including Docklands, the Dry Dock area, the Pile Yard, and even the site in Geelong housing the Museum there, were examined.

However, one site stood out above all — the area recently vacated by the Port of Melbourne Authority at Williamstown. It was, and still is, one of the best sites in the world for a Maritime Museum. The area had come under the control of the State Department known as Parks Victoria and it was with this body that we were forced to negotiate.

The site includes wharves, slipways, several old sheds that dated back to the Iron Building period, and a major building that originally housed many different trade activities connected to running a major seaport. The cost of maintaining these features, especially the wharves, is still an enormous burden on the State, and has to be considered in any future planning.

Initial plans for the site had been submitted by a commercial group, and this included a mix of historical and profitable enterprises. This was prepared at great cost, but was finally rejected by Parks for some unknown political reason.

When we came on the scene we had a rival. At this time a local group, the Williamstown Maritime Association, had been formed. Their main objective was to promote local history and the trades and people involved. Their membership was made up of local residents who volunteered their time to update and maintain the site, and their message to Parks was that instead of the State Government financing a 40 Million Dollars State Museum, they could take over the development and upkeep of the site at no cost to the public purse.

Parks Victoria proved clever at playing each of us off against each other for some time. We fought for political support, pointing out that other States had made similar investments for less conspicuous sites, but it was a losing battle.

The State had recently supported the formation of a group comprising small museums built around local history and events, known collectively as the Victorian Maritime Museum, with the ambition of promoting tourism around Victoria. It was an ambitious scheme, but nowhere did it include our objective of telling the history of seafaring, and the part ships and sailors played in the growth of Australia or its part in peace and war.

The writing was on the wall. All our efforts seemed in vain, and especially when a group calling themselves Seaworks, and consisting mainly of those previously involved with land development, were granted a long lease over the site, with their promises to develop the area into a profitable operation.

That was years ago, and we still waiting for a successful outcome. The only parts of the site that are worth mentioning are a very worthwhile and popular Museum, run by volunteers but without any encouragement or even recognition from the Seaworks' Board, and the section known as the Pirates' Tavern. This is operated by members of the WMA, but operates without a lease from the Seaworks Board, and lives therefore on a day-to-day basis.

To me, the whole set up of Seaworks and its ongoing existence is incredible. The Board has nobody on it with a real maritime background. The chairman was a well-known yachtsman and one of the Directors spent a limited time as a non-seaman rating in the R.A.N. There have been a few short-term leases granted, and Grants have been received from the State for some improvements, but the only activities organised by Seaworks themselves have been any items which have nothing to with the sea, such as Car Shows, Lego Exhibitions, etc.

The Museum is well run and admired by the few visitors but is ready for exploitation. It is open only for a few hours each week, and their work with schools is very limited. It relies only on a limited group of volunteers, and seems to have no support from the Seawork's Board. It has a wonderful collection of models.

The Pirates' Tavern is only 'tolerated' by the Board, though the main activities and the Bar sponsored by them have become a fixture in Williamstown social life even without a Lease.

It is possible that the newly appointed Manager, and also a part-time education specialist, may make vital changes, but as at March 2020, there has been little progress and its main areas of success seem to be only on a temporary basis.

I wish the project well, but I fear the wrong people are in charge at the moment.

When the situation with MHAV became intolerable, the future prospects were uncertain, and the Membership dwindled to virtually nothing, it was decided to wind it up. Some members tried to be persuaded into believing that by the support given finally to Seaworks, some of the original objectives had been achieved. I feel that this is wishful thinking.

At the final meeting of the MHAV, where the resolution

was passed to wind up the Association, it was also decided that any artefacts on loan to Seaworks would be given to them unreservedly, and that any funds remaining in the Bank account would be given as a donation to Seaworks.

To me this was a sad ending for something that started with so much promise. One point is obvious in retrospect. That the success of any venture, if it requires public funding, would come only with political influence. That was one thing we lacked once Sir Rupert Hamer passed away and it was never replaced.

51. Starlab & Teaching Astronomy.

I suppose this final episode in my life started when my ex-wife Tracy said to me "You don't need all this nonsense, Charley"

This was when I reached home tired and stressed after a particularly difficult Board Meeting at the Polly Woodside. The Directors were old cronies of the Chairman from the 'Big End of Town' and had constantly criticised my simple accounting systems. Unsophisticated as they were, we knew where we were commercially soon after the end of each month, whereas they were happy to wait months, for pure figures.

I had been at the place as CEO for over eleven years, and was nearly 60 years old. In addition to the problems with this new Board, I had become sick of the way politicians and others were taking the credit for the restoration of the ship, when it was the many volunteers that should have been given the praise.

They had donated their time and worked so hard from the early days, even before I went there. It was really their efforts that had turned the old coal hulk into a fine sailing ship, not those who now wanted the praise. It was all done on a shoe-string, thanks to the small staff and the volunteers who gave their time and skills free, plus the many Melbourne companies who donated rope, steel, timber, and services. Politicians had done nothing, and were now heard to say "Look what we have done!"

I had built up many contacts throughout the Education and Tourism sectors, and saw opportunities in these areas. Therefore, I resigned from the National Trust, and formed a new company that I called Journeyman Tours Pty. Ltd, later trading as Journeyman Education services.

My first venture was under the banner of "Melbourne Pride" inspired by the late Noel Coward, whose song "London Pride" was a hit during WW2. The basis of this business was to teach the history of our great City, and then create a franchise network for the other Australian main cities.

In the midst of these preparations, my mother in the UK sent me an SOS about my step-father's sickness, and I flew to be with her in London. This emergency passed, but I took the chance to meet a few ship-mates, and so it happened that I had lunch aboard HMS Chrysanthemum, an ex- Q ship from WW1 and then permanently tied-up alongside the Westminster Embankment. This ship was run by a school support group, called Interaction, and their work was partly financed by running a restaurant aboard the ship.

During lunch I met their Manager. We discussed mutual

work with schools, and I was invited to see their portable planetarium, which turned out to be an inflatable dome, of about six meters in diameter and inflated by a large electric fan.

Starlab — The Portable Planetarium

So this was how I was introduced to "Starlab" as it was called. I entered this fascinating dome, the night sky was switched on, and I was spellbound. In a flash I knew that this was where my future lay, and all the astronomy that I had learnt as a maritime navigator would be the foundation of my future career.

I found that Starlab had been invented by an American teacher at a school in Boston, who had believed that there had to be a better way of teaching Astronomy in the classroom. He had made a prototype from plastic bags and a household fan, and then set up a company for making the product.

I telephoned Boston that evening, and arranged to fly there within a few days for discussions. My aim was to secure 'Starlab' as an exclusive Agency for Australia and New Zealand, and subsequent negotiations with Mr. Phil Sadler, the inventor, achieved this. The appointment meant purchasing a Starlab unit and providing sufficient working capital for advertising and setting up the business. This absorbed all of my savings and most of the superannuation that I had accrued during my time at the Polly Woodside, but nothing diminished my excitement about the new venture.

There was a two month time delay before the equipment arrived, and simultaneously but unknown to me at the time, it had been decided that the State Planetarium in the City would be converted into the State Library, and the Planetarium moved to the new Science Museum at Spotswood. During the three year period that the planning and the construction of the Planetarium took, my Starlab would therefore be the only resource available to schools and the public to learn about basic astronomy.

As a result I was given a part-time contract as an in-house lecturer at the Science Museum during this period, and it also gave me an opportunity for the schools to learn the benefits that a portable unit could afford them. It also gave me the time to finalise all my lessons, and to bring my teaching into line with the State curriculum for all student grades.

I decided then, and forever, that we would stick to every-day astronomy, things that happened to all of us, and not to pretend that we knew all about deep space. At that time there was interest in exploring the Solar System, and I was intrigued that the same problems to be overcome; things like food, communication, and navigation in their endeavours, were what early explorers on earth and at sea, similar to Columbus in the fifteenth century, had to also overcome.

51. Starlab & Teaching Astronomy.

Because of the demand for knowledge and our service, I very quickly had three units on the road and was forced to employ two other science teachers. I realise in hindsight that I could have made more profit than I did, but I was conscious that I would soon be competing with a State-run facility, and would have to keep it tight.

A trip to Chickamauga — In Georgia

Every year that I worked as the agent for the portable planetarium Starlab, I would attend the annual conference at the manufacturer's factory in the city of Boston, Massachusetts, and then combine this with other visits to other places in the USA and Europe.

I looked forward to these conferences each year, shared with other delegates from each part of the United States and from various parts of Europe. Although of differing nationalities we all had a common interest in education and astronomy, and many friendships were born.

Whatever year this was, Australia had recently won the Americas Cup yacht race (The first time the Americans had been beaten in over 100 years of sailing matches) and a Vegemite Sandwich featured in the famous Australian team signature tune "The men from Down-Under." I had therefore taken a bottle of this mysterious, salty black stuff, hitherto unknown in the USA, for everybody round the conference table to try. I can recall the resultant faces of horror afterwards.

One particular year, I was to be a guest of NASA at Houston in Texas, so I accepted an invitation to stay a few days with Jim and Shirley Smith at Chickamauga in Georgia on the way. They were both ex-secondary school teachers and were Starlab agents for that part of USA.

The small town of Chickamauga is near Chattanooga, and both places were famous for frantic battles during the American Civil War, where casualties on both sides were unbelievable. I found that the Civil War was still being fought in some communities, with the Confederate flag still quite prominent. Statues in memory of the regiments of both sides were erected, and the old wooden shed used as a first aid post was still standing.

With both Jim and Shirley avid historians, it proved to be a most interesting visit, touring these battle areas featured in the history of the United States.

However, at breakfast on the second day of my visit, Jim announced that before sight-seeing we were to witness the retrieval of a time capsule buried by Jim's father under the concrete foundations of the local school's planetarium in 1949. The planetarium was to be renewed, and the concrete pad was to be broken up, and that the Time Capsule was to be lifted.

We arrived at the scene to find a jack hammer and bulldozer already at work, with a group of workers standing-by. When told of the parcel to be found, the workers were convinced that they were to witness the final saga of a bank robbery or some similar crime. Their excitement was obvious and mounting.

Eventually, the parcel was found. It was a cube of about

a meter in size, dark and mysterious. It was wrapped in layers of black plastic, which when removed it proved to be covering several metal ammunition cases. Because of the anticipation for discovering the contents, there was no shortage of volunteers to prise open the rusty lids.

The faces of those expecting a rich find were a picture of disappointment. Instead of ill-gotten gains, the contents turned out to be a collection of Holy Bibles, printed in every language found throughout the whole world.

Jim explained. His father was an ardent Baptist lay preacher, and in common with many Americans at that time, was convinced that the United States would be invaded and conquered by the Communists of Eastern Europe, and that they would afterwards ban all types of religious practice. He had arranged that these Bibles would be buried so at least they and Christianity would endure.

Opening the Time Capsule

These Bibles were put in boot of Jim's car, and we left the disgruntled workers disappointed, and grumbling among themselves that they had been misled to provide their labour for no purpose.

The Business Grew

As we grew and became more and more accepted by the schools, we tried many different avenues of expansion, but it was the concentration on basic astronomy that was our main success. This was assisted to no small degree by the dedication of our staff. First was Mark Hanny, who had studied to become a priest until he fell for a lovely girl, and the two of them left for New Zealand. His place was filled by a first class teacher, Lyn O'Halloran, who was with me for eleven years, as a friend and advisor. Lyn only left us because it seemed that the business would be sold.

This was how we entered the market, and how the business developed. Although we were responsible for selling Starlab units though-out the whole of Australia and New Zealand, we kept the teaching operation in Victoria to ourselves, and apart from a few schools in southern NSW, we serviced only schools in Victoria.

I found out the difficulties of operating in Education. With the long school holidays, it meant that only about 34 weeks per year were available, and even these were restricted by short terms and exams. I also quickly found out that to employ well trained and qualified teachers was a drain on financial resources and yet to employ casual teachers led to a performance and reliability problem.

As a remedy, we offered public astronomy session to shopping centres and to holiday programs, and this quickly helped us to develop a wider range of clients and subjects. While it helped the problem to some degree, it never completely did so in the whole time we ran the business.

Mirror Projection — Formation of Cosmodome.

The standard Starlab projection system consisted of a special projector fitted with a very small (and very expensive) light bulb over which was fitted a series of plastic cylinders, especially computorized to project onto the dome. It was very similar in concept to a nursery toy I bought for my daughter. Of these cylinders the Night Sky range of stars (known as the Star Field) and the map of the World were the most outstanding, but there were many different cylinders to choose from.

These projections were ideal for our school work, but even though we augmented them with photo-slides and video clips, and while those were really the first innovation in the world to Starlab, they had only limited interest for entertaining the general public at shopping centres.

A lifeboat came in sight, thanks to Swinburne University

in 2005. Up to that time, movies could only be projected on to a 360 degree dome by means of a special fish-eye lens, which was very expensive

Because we had smaller inflatable domes, we were invited to work with them on the development of a new system called Mirrordome, which finally became known as "Mirror Projection". This involved replacing the fish-eye lens by a curved mirror and a smaller projector, resulting in much lower capital cost and with greater suitability for smaller domes. It also had the added advantage in that the equipment was placed at the edge of the dome, rather than at the centre giving greater audience space and better viability.

The Cosmodome

It took a while for the final product to be marketable, and finally we were appointed as Market Agents and formed Cosmodome Australia Pty. Ltd. to handle this. We began introducing and selling Mirrodome all over the world, buying licenced units and other equipment from Swinburne, and selling via sub-agents in USA and Europe. Eventually we were faced with severe competition within USA, our major sales area, when we found to our horror that the system had not been patented by Swinburne and we were beaten by money.

Overseas sales tapered off, but Cosmodome films gave us additional features for our school and holiday offerings. We built up quite a library of educational and children's films, to either show or sell and this helped maintain our local viability.

From this time onwards, we offered schools either the Starlab lecture with supporting slides or clips, or a Cosmodome movie of their choice. Most of the movies lasted for about 30 minutes, so both programmes ended with a study of the night sky, with planets, and the constellations.

As the movie range widened, we were able to add new lessons to our range, such as weather, aboriginal astronomy, natural disasters, and other areas of science. For the school holidays we added movies aimed at children, and also seasonal items such as Christmas Carols or the Christmas Star.

We also tried to diversify, and I was helped in this by

51. Starlab & Teaching Astronomy.

my old friend Miles Allen. We introduced the Party Dome, which could hold six children and would fit into a carport. Then came the open-fronted Show Dome aimed at the Gaming or exhibition markets. These were good products, but failed because of marketing difficulties, money, or too high running costs.

This was also the problem with our new Spaceworks. This was introduced when eventually the Planetarium at Science Works came on stream, and demand for Starlab reduced. This project was aimed at keeping the Starlab operators, both teachers, employed. We invented two programmes, Astronaut Training and Planet Exploration. The two teachers did an excellent job in preparing those programmes, and we spent much capital in producing various products to be used.

It has to be said that I did not do sufficient home-work, and once launched, we found that we could only handle about two classes of students per day, and we had severely under-costed the presentations. Try as we might, viability could not be achieved, and we had to stop the drain on our limited resources. I was forced to lay off these special teachers and call a halt to the programmes.

Throughout the whole 22 years that I ran this business I was fortunate in having wonderful and dedicated staff. We always remained a very small team, and I felt they were all my family. I employed science teachers, though very few had a background in astronomy. In fact, this lack showed me a weakness in our educational system, and the need to train more specialised teachers, particularly in maths and science, or the STEM subjects as they are now called.

2. Retirement

I gave up actually teaching when I found that my advancing age had undermined my sense of balance, and I found that if for any reason I fell over in the dome, it was only with difficulty that I could re-again my feet. From then on, I simply concentrated on running the business, taking the bookings by email or over the phone, and doing general accounting work.

Paperwork has never been my strongpoint and it actually bored me. I missed the children and their shining thirst for knowledge, and missed even the daily exercise of moving the equipment from the car each morning and loading it back at the end of the day.

Eventually, I decided to sell the business, a decision I should have taken much earlier. I negotiated the sale with one of the science teachers that was working for me and was a personal friend. At the same time, I sold my house at Hoppers Crossing, and moved back to Williamstown, where I had anyway spent most of my leisure time, because of membership at a local Yacht Club. I found then that even the Marina was too much for my limited mobility, and sold my yacht.

51. Starlab & Teaching Astronomy.

I can really say that at an age of over eighty, this was an inevitable end to the long and varied story of my Life. I fought a rear-guard action by forming a new business, but soon realised that I had to face facts and that this was a really pitiful attempt to put off the inevitable, All I had left was to write my memoirs, and that now is my main motivation. The problem with that is that it is all a question of looking back, whereas I have spent my life ignoring the past and just looking ahead.

I have to accept — The Sun is setting.

www.ingramcontent.com/pod-product-compliance
Lightning Source LLC
Chambersburg PA
CBHW031230290426
44109CB00012B/237